1970

This book may be k

THAILAND: ANOTHER VIETNAM?

Thailand:
Another Vietnam?

❧ DANIEL WIT
Northern Illinois University

CHARLES SCRIBNER'S SONS
New York

To my wife, Phyllis

PREFACE

In Thailand, America has gained an ally which is a vigorous proponent of our role as an Asian power and stabilizer. It is also a proud and independent country whose centuries of independence and of freedom from colonialism probably make it as completely and uncorruptedly Asian as any land on that continent. Thailand is no subservient "lackey" of any foreign power and, unlike many of the much more artificial countries of the contemporary non-Western world, there is a historic Thai way-of-life which has been developing continuously for almost a thousand recorded years. It is the hope of this writer that in the contemporary Thai-American alliance will be found one of the most mutually fruitful associations of East and West yet established—an association in which both partners are able to pursue their national self-interests and retain their integrity to their own and Southeast Asia's advantage.

I would like to thank Miss Barbara Anderson and Mrs. Marge Speer for their conscientious and efficient typing of the manuscript. To my wife as well as to my children, Pam and Fred, go endless thanks both for their love and companionship during our residence in Thailand and elsewhere in the world and for their continuous encouragement in regard to this particular manuscript. My thanks, too, to Professor Harold W. Chase, Scribners political science advisory editor for his support, understanding and helpfulness.

DANIEL WIT

DeKalb, Illinois

CONTENTS

THAILAND: ANOTHER VIETNAM?

CHAPTER I

❦

Thailand and the Challenge of Revolutionary Warfare

An American Ally Under Pressure

"We hope to have a guerrilla war in Thailand before the year is out," declared Communist China's Foreign Minister, Chen Yi, toward the end of 1965. Since then a small but active guerrilla campaign has steadily grown in Thailand as an adjunct of Communist revolutionary warfare in the neighboring lands of Southeast Asia. Thailand, therefore, has now joined Laos, Vietnam, Malaysia, Indonesia, the Philippines, Cambodia and even pro-Peking and neutralist Burma[1] as a target of this new imperialism whose assaults appear to ebb and flow with varying degrees of

[1] After a long period of pointing to Burma (which had virtually severed relations with the West in order to appease Red China) as an outstanding example of its friendly relationships with border countries, Peking published on July 10, 1967, a statement of full sympathy for a "revolutionary people's war" to overthrow the Burmese government. It suddenly described the latter as a fascist regime of "greedy blood-soakers" which served imperialist interests and was "doomed to destruction . . . the armed revolution, led by the Burmese Communist Party, represents the developmental orientation of the people of Burma."

intensity, depending upon prevailing regional conditions and the opportunities offered.

The open Chinese commitment to the overthrow of Thailand's government came as no surprise to the Thai leadership or to serious professional students of Chinese Communist foreign policy. After all, as four distinguished Princeton professors have noted in an authorized study for Senator Fulbright's Foreign Relations Committee, Communist China "has pronounced it to be its duty as a revolutionary power to support 'wars of liberation,' that is, to abet Communist and 'anti-imperialist' revolution anywhere. To the present Chinese leaders, revolutionary war knows no territorial limitations." [2] In the case of Southeast Asia, to quote from an addendum to the same Senate study—prepared at Senator Lausche's (Ohio) request: "Peking's ultimate goal is that Burma, Thailand, Laos, Cambodia and Malaysia—like North Vietnam—come under the rule of Communist parties which pursue domestic and foreign policies consonant with those of China. Peking also expects that these Communist governments will come to power using the techniques of armed struggle developed in China's own Communist revolution." [3]

In applying its revolutionary warfare policy to Thailand—the only Southeast Asian country to escape colonialism and one with 700 years of national independence—Red China started a propaganda campaign against the Thai government as early as 1950 (the Communists captured control of China only in October of 1949). Its justification was the alleged oppression of Chinese residents in Thailand. This was then expanded, with active Soviet cooperation, into a wider effort to win over Thai intellectuals to the Communist new order or at least to a neutralist foreign policy. So threatening, from the Thai leadership's viewpoint, had these

[2] *Neutralization in Southeast Asia: Problems and Prospects*, A Study Prepared at the Request of the Committee on Foreign Relations, United States Senate (by Professors Cyril E. Black, Richard A. Falk, Klaus Knorr, and Oran Young), dated October 10, 1966 (Washington, D.C.: U.S. Government Printing Office, 1966), p. 14.

[3] *Ibid.*, p. 36.

efforts become by 1952 that the government, confronted with evidence of Communist success in capturing the sympathies of part of its large Chinese minority (about 10 percent of the population and almost 50 percent of Bangkok), conducted mass raids and arrested several hundred Chinese. The Thai police claimed that they had uncovered a Communist plot to seize the country. Later investigations revealed that many ethnic Thai were also involved in some form of plotting, although the actual extent of Communist infiltration was uncertain. Subsequently, in January of 1953, Peking proclaimed the creation in South China (Yunnan province) of a Thai Autonomous People's Government, whose purpose would be to guide other neighboring Thai-speaking people in the struggle against Western "imperialist" oppression. Although most of the Thai people had fled south into the Indo-Chinese peninsula during the twelfth and thirteenth centuries in the wake of military defeat by the Mongol lords of China, some had remained behind and become incorporated into the Chinese Empire. By this new pseudo Pan-Thaism, the Chinese obviously were creating yet another instrument with which to promote the shattering of contemporary Thailand.[4]

From the Thai perspective, these early Chinese Communist propaganda and political maneuvers to disrupt Thai unity and to pressure the country into a neutralist foreign policy began to take on an even more ominous character as a result of Communist guerrilla and conventional warfare successes in neighboring Vietnam and Laos. For, with adaptations to local conditions and with Chinese advice and assistance, the general Maoist model for revolutionary warfare was being applied throughout the former French Indo-Chinese empire with significant results. The progressive stages of that model, based on Mao's experience in capturing mainland China, call for (1) creation of a local elitist and conspiratorial Communist party, (2) expansion of the party's effective influence through infiltration and then association of "popular"

[4] See Donald E. Nuechterlein, *Thailand and the Struggle for Southeast Asia* (Ithaca, N.Y.: Cornell University Press, 1965), pp. 110–112.

mass elements (workers, peasants, intellectuals), with its policies, (3) vigorous agitational activities and capture of control of bourgeois groups, (4) actual launching of military attacks upon the existing government in a series of defined escalations from guerrilla to eventually conventional uses of armed force, (5) ultimate overthrow of the government and, on the heels of military victory, establishment of a "People's Democracy".[5]

Highlights of what successive Thai governments have witnessed with growing alarm in neighboring lands and at home are:

(1) Vietminh victory over the French, which led in 1954 to the creation of an actual Communist North Vietnamese state;

(2) Active Vietminh-North Vietnamese help for the Pathet Lao Communist movement, which was subordinated to Hanoi and coordinated with the latter's own campaign first against the French and then against South Vietnam;[6]

(3) Increasing Pathet Lao success in capturing control, by 1954, of up to two-thirds of the territory of the new state of Laos, which borders on Thailand;

(4) Periodic Pathet Lao attempts to take over all of Laos between 1954 and 1965 while binding their occupied territories directly to China and North Vietnam through new roads and air transportation;

(5) Mounting Pathet Lao and North Vietnamese infiltration into Northeast Thailand since 1963 in order to promote separatism among the eight million Thai of Lao ethnic origin (there are actually only about one millon Lao living on the other side of the Mekong River in Laos);

(6) Chinese establishment in early 1965 of a United Patriotic Front of Thailand and a Thai Independence Movement (plus other more specialized professional and occupational subversive groups), which were then merged in November 1965 to create a

[5] See Robert A. Scalapino, ed., *The Communist Revolution in Asia* (Englewood Cliffs, N.J.: Prentice-Hall, Inc., 1965), pp. 16–22.
[6] See Bernard Fall, "The Pathet Lao," *ibid.*, pp. 178–179.

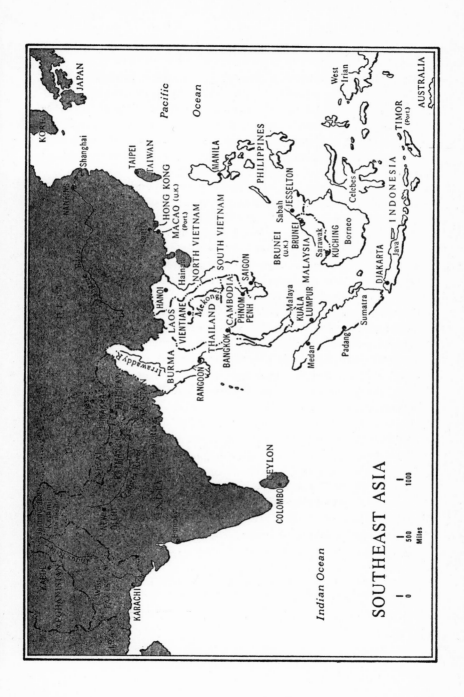

SOUTHEAST ASIA

Thai Patriotic Front to lead the avowed campaign to capture Thailand;

(7) Separatist and guerrilla activities in Thailand's four southern provinces (80 percent of whose population are of Malay ethnic extraction) bordering on Malaya, by several hundred outlawed members of the Malayan Communist movement, in order to place Thailand in a guerrilla warfare nutcracker;

(8) A growing pattern in Northeast Thailand of terrorist assassinations of local Thai officials, ambushes of police, and propagandizing of villages, a pattern which resembles the early stages of Communist guerrilla warfare in Laos and Vietnam.

In response to this revolutionary warfare campaign launched against it by Peking and Hanoi, the Thai government has not sought to save itself through appeasement of Communism. Unlike Cambodia's Prince Sihanouk, whose policy Thai Foreign Minister Thanat Khoman has described as being that of "facing the crocodile and trying to be the last to be eaten," the Thai government has chosen to resist and to fight back in open alliance with the United States. The Chinese Foreign Minister's 1965 declaration that Thailand was next on the list as a target for Communist "national liberation" warfare prompted Mr. Thanat to characterize it as

> amounting to a declaration of war. When a country says against another country that "we will start a war," be it a guerrilla war or an open war, it doesn't make much difference. It has been a declaration of war on the part of Communist China on Thailand. Now, of course, it is guerrilla war, and we are taking necessary measures and steps to meet the situation.[7]

This frank and determined response is indicative of the various foreign policy actions taken by Thailand since 1950.[8] Among

---

[7] Thanat Khoman, *Report from Southeast Asia,* issued in May 1965 by the Permanent Mission of Thailand to the United Nations, New York, N.Y.

[8] See Nuechterlein, for a complete analysis of Thai foreign policy.

the highlights to be noted in Thailand's post-World War II search for national security are these:

(1) An initial and unsuccessful effort was made (under the Pridi government) during 1946 and 1947 to mediate the French conflict with the Vietminh. This was followed by a proposal that France and Thailand jointly sponsor a Southeast Asian Union whose core would be the free states of Laos, Cambodia, and Vietnam, but with which other Southeast Asian countries might also eventually associate themselves. The French rejected this proposal in behalf of a policy of seeking military victory over the Vietminh rather than of promoting real Indo-Chinese independence.

(2) From 1948 to 1950, a "wait and see" policy was adopted (under the Phibun government) concerning the thrust and meaning of the still confused and overlapping Communist and nationalist revolutions occuring throughout all the rest of Southeast Asia. The Thai government was sympathetic to the national aspirations for independence among its neighbors but suspicious of Communist goals.

(3) When the full significance and objectives of Communism in Southeast Asia had become clear by 1950—their desire to capture and then pervert the local nationalist and anti-colonialist movements—Thailand (under Phibun) made a conscious policy decision to join the West and particularly the United States in resisting this threat to the national independence of the Southeast Asian peoples.

(4) With both pro-Communism and neutralism rejected, Thailand proceeded to enter into agreements with the United States for both Economic and Technical Cooperation (September 1950) and Military Assistance (October 1950). These agreements were followed by (a) active participation alongside the United States in the Korean War (Thailand provided rice plus several thousand troops); (b) open condemnation before the United Nations of the 1953 and 1954 Vietminh invasions of Laos and Cambodia and related threats to Thai security; (c) entry into the American-sponsored SEATO pact of September 1954 (although

it should be noted that the Thai wanted SEATO to be more like NATO and include automatic guarantees of collective military aid to countries attacked); (d) calls for SEATO to give firm security guarantees to South Vietnam, Laos, and Cambodia; (e) strong appeals to SEATO and the United States from 1958 on to prevent any Communist take-over in Laos (under the Thanom, Sarit, and second Thanom governments); (f) public declarations by Thai leaders of a determination to fight alone, if necessary, if the Pathet Lao Communists actually took over all of Laos; (g) indication of willingness to receive American armed forces and permit the creation of joint military base areas on Thai territory. This latter step was taken both to counter Pathet Lao actions across the border and to facilitate American military efforts (by air) to interdict the Ho Chi Minh supply trail through Laos to South Vietnam as well as to strike at North Vietnam.

Since 1950, therefore, Thailand has become America's only Southeast Asian mainland ally (other than South Vietnam). It has also been an ally which has, if anything, been even firmer and less equivocating than the United States in its identification of the Communist security threat to the region. It has openly based its own security upon the United States; urged an American military presence in Southeast Asia as the only means of containing the Peking- and Hanoi-sponsored revolutionary wars; castigated "neutralization" as meaning that "you may get peace for six months and then afterwards you have to endure the yoke of Communist colonialism as a tool of their power";[9] and, strategically, has compared the contemporary Southeast Asian situation with that facing Europe when Hitler sought to take over the Rhineland: "If the expanding power of the Asian Communist is not stopped, it is most likely that another war—and a large scale war—might happen. . . . What would happen if the United States and other free nations in the world withdrew from Southeast Asia and left the field open to the Communists? The Communists would take over South

[9] Thanat Khoman.

10

Vietnam, go to Laos, Cambodia, Burma, Thailand, and then move on and on and on." [10]

Yet despite this strong support for the American role and presence in Southeast Asia—in fact, because of it—Thailand also constitutes an important foreign policy problem for the United States. America, with its global concerns and responsibilities as well as with one very hot war on its hands in Southeast Asia, faces the real possibility that its activist Thai ally may also become engulfed by Communist revolutionary warfare. Peking and Hanoi have made a start in this direction and have openly proclaimed their goal to be the capture of Thailand. America is pledged to help defend Thailand not just under the SEATO pact but also on a bilateral basis following a joint statement issued by Secretary of State Dean Rusk and Thai Foreign Minister Thanat Khoman on March 6, 1962, after Mr. Thanat had met with and received a similar verbal assurance from President Kennedy. That statement declared:

> The Secretary of State reaffirmed that the United States regards the preservation of the independence and integrity of Thailand as vital to the national interest of the United States and to world peace. He expressed the firm intention of the United States to aid Thailand, its ally and historic friend, in resisting Communist aggression and subversion. . . . The Secretary of State reaffirmed that this obligation of the United States does not depend upon the prior agreement of all other parties to the Treaty [SEATO], since this Treaty obligation is individual as well as collective.[11]

This commitment of the United States to Thailand has caused important senators like Fulbright and Morse to ask publicly, as the former did in hearings of his Senate Foreign Relations Committee during January of 1967: "[Are we] in Thailand . . . preparing another Vietnam? . . . We have an investment of hundreds of

---

[10] *Ibid.*
[11] *Department of State Bulletin,* March 26, 1962, p. 498.

millions of dollars in enormous bases . . . with an enormous combination naval air base. What effect does this activity have upon the future stability of Thailand and upon our commitment?" For Senator Fulbright, who has made it clear that he believes our involvement in Vietnam to have been unwise, the question about Thailand becomes: "Do you foresee any similar development growing out of a commitment in Thailand from our point of view?" [12] Obviously, it is the fear of the Chairman of the Senate Foreign Relations Committee—as well as of some other concerned Americans—that Thailand may become another Vietnam and that this would be disastrous for the United States. Since the Thai themselves assert that all of Southeast Asia has to be viewed as an interrelated whole, this is not a meaningless question to pose. It is particularly worthwhile to pose it at what is still a relatively early stage.

But how does one go about answering the question of whether Thailand is another potential Vietnam? The remainder of this book is an effort to do so by bringing to bear on the problem what we now know of the scope and depth of Communist revolutionary warfare and what we also know about the totality of Thailand as a society. Only by examining the problem in this way can one do more than provide superficial answers to a question with historic implications for the entire American role as a power in Southeast Asia.

Revolutionary Wars and the Way to Win Them

The Communist-proclaimed "wars of national liberation" which have been waged since the end of World War II are basically revolutionary wars of a special type. The Western use of such older labels as "insurgency" and "guerrilla war" does not reflect their real scope and objectives. The very narrowness and shallow-

---

[12] *Asia, the Pacific and the United States,* Hearings before the Committee on Foreign Relations, U.S. Senate, 90th Cong., 1st Sess. with former Ambassador to Japan, Edwin O. Reischauer, January 31, 1967, p. 66.

ness of these labels is misleading, for they do not suggest what the Communists have added to these very ancient forms of conflict. After all, ancient Rome and China, like many other pre-modern states, also experienced insurgencies and guerrilla actions, as did Napoleon, the American Union forces during the Civil War, nineteenth-century America in the Indian uprisings, Nazi Germany in the case of the various partisans groups, etc. While these struggles share some basic characteristics with today's unconventional warfare, they also differ in some very important respects.

In the many cases of irregular warfare which can be cited throughout history, there generally have been several outstanding characteristics which continue to exist in the current conflicts:

(1) The insurgents and guerrillas normally were inferior to their opponents in regular (conventional) military might, which was usually why they employed this form of warfare;

(2) Their motivations were psychological and ideological, which distinguished them from mere bandits—they were frustrated by existing social, economic and/or political conditions, had little hope of achieving their aspirations and dreams of a better society under the existing political regime, and so felt oppressed;

(3) Their hopes of success in gaining their objectives by resort to force depended mainly on their ability either to wear down and politically divide a regime to the point where it collapsed from within or, eventually, to convert themselves into regular conventional forces capable of defeating the regime militarily.

To these classic characteristics, the Communists have added major changes in doctrine, strategy, and tactics in order to make such warfare revolutionary in the twentieth-century context. Some understanding both of its specific Communist and of its twentieth-century substance, therefore, is essential in order to know how to deal with contemporary revolutionary warfare in Thailand or anywhere else.

To begin with, in the twentieth century, unconventional warfare like conventional warfare has become "popularized," a result of the steady expansion of mass participation in war since the eighteenth century. It is a product of the greater dependence of "popular" uprisings on irregular uses of violence in order to circumvent the greatly enhanced technological and organizational instruments available to a government's regular armed forces. Moreover, it is in tune with the new and steadily rising aspirations of millions of people in Asia, Africa, the Middle East, and Latin America for more personal dignity, more sense of participation in a politics which dominates their lives to a far greater extent than in the past, more economic well-being, and more varied opportunities for the individual and his children to develop themselves to the limits of their inherent capabilities. The mid-twentieth century is, after all, a revolutionary era.

Within this twentieth-century mass revolutionary context, the Communists have launched a campaign of "protracted warfare" which is based upon their own particular ideological perspective. Viewing historic progress as a "natural" product of inevitable socio-economic class conflict, and identifying the contemporary enemies of such progress toward their particular version of utopia as the "Western capitalist imperialists" and their non-Western "puppets," they have believed themselves to be morally justified in employing all available means at their disposal to overthrow their historic foes. They have openly proclaimed their desire to "bury" in one way or another what they call capitalist imperialism.

Given Communist totalitarianism, this perspective has produced a highly integrated and developed strategy as well as a highly coordinated system of conflict management. The struggle is waged in all sectors of society, at all levels of violence, and over an extended period of time, if such is required in order to prevent their own destruction by more conventionally powerful opponents. It is full of "zigs" and "zags," offensive and defensive tactics, advances and retreats; and it involves the manipulation of economic, social, ideological, scientific-technological, and violence factors by a tough, disciplined, and highly motivated political elite.

Although the overwhelming dominance of the Soviet Union within the Communist countries of the world and among the

Communist parties outside that "world" has been shattered—there is now a polycentrism based upon the existence of several Communist power groupings as well as a new national Communism which has enhanced the discretionary powers of Communist leaders in individual states—varying degrees of international ideological agreement and operational coordination still remain. In the specific case of Southeast Asia, we therefore find Communist North Vietnam receiving both Red Chinese and Soviet assistance in its struggle to capture South Vietnam, see evidences of Hanoi's willingness to coordinate its conduct of revolutionary warfare throughout the other former French Indo-Chinese states (Laos and Cambodia) and in Thailand with Chinese Communist foreign policy, and also have indications of Hanoi's separate national Communist desire to constitute itself as a source of Communist leadership on the Indo-Chinese peninsula, apart from the national foreign policies of Peking and Moscow.

The actual strategy for waging Communist revolutionary wars, as noted earlier, leans heavily upon Maoist doctrine. That doctrine identifies specific stages in a campaign's development, including the pertinent tactics to be followed. It involves a process of planned escalation which moves (1) from the initial preparation of a target society by infiltration and subversion (2) to the inauguration of guerrilla warfare, the establishment of "base" areas within the country under assault, the subsequent creation of regular mobile military forces, and ultimately (3) to conventional military victory (in association with continued guerrilla warfare) over a regime which has lost its popular support, any internal political unity it may have had, and even its original military superiority. This entire process, from start to finish, is to be conducted under the tight control of Communist political leadership and in behalf of ideological and political objectives. It is, moreover, heavily dependent upon the gaining of some mass (but not necessarily majority) support, sympathy, or at least acquiescence through a combination of positive appeals (psychological, political and socio-economic) and selective use of terrorism. When conducted in overwhelmingly agrarian societies (the characteristic society of almost all non-Western countries), this revolutionary warfare campaign is also geared primarily to the indigenous peasantry and seeks to pit it against both landlords and urban "capitalists." It is this type of assault which has now begun in Thailand. It is this complex challenge, and not just that implied by "guerrilla war," to which the Thai government and its American ally must devise an effective response if the country is not to become another Vietnam. But what sort of response can one really devise? Is it not just a matter of the government's being able to exercise overwhelming military force?

On the contrary, the most effective counter to Communist revolutionary warfare involves, rather than military force, the early elimination of those internal stresses and weaknesses of society on which "national liberation" wars feed, in combination with the provision of adequate physical security to the members of a target society. Revolutionary warfare attempts cannot easily get off the ground and beyond Maoist stage one if a nation is united behind its government and if there is no significant degree of popular discontent, frustration, or alienation from the regime in power. Terrorism and subversion can then be handled by a good internal police and security system, which is provided with the necessary intelligence information by a basically loyal populace. It can actually be reduced to mere banditry as even the would-be revolutionaries come to realize that they have no cause to which people will rally. Under such circumstances, the foreign sponsors of guerrillas and insurgents face the necessity either of withdrawing support and accepting failure, or of attempting an open conventional military invasion. The latter, being more easily identifiable, can also be more easily condemned throughout the world and effectively resisted as old-fashioned aggression. Claims about the conflict being a local civil war or a popular uprising against an oppressive regime can clearly be seen for the falsehood they are. Obviously, "counter-insurgency" efforts by a government are much easier in this atmosphere than they are after real guerrilla warfare has begun and been sustained with a measure of popular support in the name of nationalism and with the proclaimed objectives of eliminating societal evils which actually do exist.

To establish and maintain an atmosphere unfavorable to Communist revolutionary warfare in the mid-twentieth century requires, however, that a country be developing rather than that it be stagnating in traditionalism or otherwise retrogressing and decaying.[13] A society is, after all, neither a mere agglommeration of disparate individuals and groups nor a concentration camp. It is an action system whose primary justification for existence is its ability to solve certain major collective problems in accordance with the vital needs and aspirations of its members. Failure to engage in the necessary problem-solving, or concern only for the desires of limited portions of a populace combined with consistent frustration of other key components, or of the majority of a society, obviously are conducive to revolutionary warfare.

If there are any universally proclaimed goals of mankind today, they are the goals of freedom, equality, dignity, social justice, material well-being, and sense of effective participation in the organizing systems of society (the political, economic, and social systems) which increasingly determine one's fate. These are mass goals. They are the goals toward which the peoples of the world increasingly desire to see their societies and their countries move. Since 1945, millions of men have been liberating themselves from colonialism with the announced objective of obtaining a major improvement in their condition in life—political, economic, social and psychological. The glory of our age is not the splendor, power, or accomplishments of various elites. The dominant ideological dynamic—regardless of various specific formulations—is populist and humanistic. A viable society (hence a viable country) is therefore necessarily one which is solving its major problems in a fashion which is in agreement with these general aspirations.

[13] See Daniel Wit, "Government and the Promotion of Development," in Clyde Wingfield, ed., *Political Science: Some New Perspectives* (El Paso: Texas Western Press, 1966), pp. 79–98, for a general discussion of the problems and requirements for development.

17

Societal viability—the capacity of a state and its society to survive and prosper without deformity in its particular environment—depends heavily on successful response to such aspirations as well as on the ability to master a particular physical environment. There may be no universally valid blueprints for structuring the organizing systems of a society since they must be "tailor-made" rather than taken off some rack containing foreign, ready-made models. Nevertheless, certain mass aspirations of the twentieth century provide universal criteria for determining whether or not a country and its government are developing. Are they solving their problems in a way which keeps moving them toward these goals? Even more specifically, are they successfully structuring their behavior patterns and their organizing systems in order to achieve the following broad characteristics of modernity—derived largely from the development of Europe and North America since the industrial revolution—which constitute essential pre-conditions for development in our age:

(1) The improved integration of a people as a nation, which provides not only the social-psychological cement necessary to their successful cooperation in pursuit of all collective goals but also makes possible the most effective use of their inherent individual and group skills, talents and energies, to that end;

(2) The expansion of meaningful mass participation in the polity, now more important than ever before because it is the political system which dominates our lives most and which also assumes the primary responsibility for the progress and development of a society;

(3) The promotion of economic growth, with resultant benefits not just to special elites and interest groups but to the masses;

(4) The improvement of the physical condition, educational level, and occupational skills of the masses, as well as of the elites, as an essential prerequisite to their becoming "modern" men in a "modern" society capable of development;

(5) The improvement of societal capabilities to employ West-

ern science and technology in order to control their physical environment better for developmental purposes;

(6) The development of capabilities for utilizing, and adapting to national objectives, those modern Western organizational forms and administrative techniques which improve decision-making and increase the effectiveness with which collective action can be taken;

(7) And, perhaps most important of all, the introduction of creative and innovative solutions to problems which are essentially of indigenous origin even though the solutions may be based upon pragmatic, eclectic, and discriminating selection from among foreign examples.

This is the context and the substance of development in our age, regardless of the specific forms of action taken or characteristics given to a society's organizing systems. Indigenous leadership must design national systems to satisfy local cultural requirements and to solve specific local problems in accordance with the universal aspirations of an age in which the masses do count and are the ultimate judges of a country's success or failure.

It is, then, the success or failure of a country and its leadership to engage in this type of development which determines its degree of receptivity to Communist revolutionary warfare or any other form of revolution. It is also, then, to an analysis in depth of Thailand's success or failure to engage in development that one must turn for any meaningful answer to Senator Fulbright's question: Will Thailand prove to be another Vietnam? Security and development are inextricably intertwined in the mid-twentieth century and both are dependent upon the quality and goals of the political system.

CHAPTER II

❀

The Making of the Thai State

Since contemporary Thailand's ability to avoid the tragedy of Vietnam is largely dependent upon its government's degree of success in resolving vital national problems and promoting national development within the context of the total Thai environment, evaluation must begin with an examination in some depth of that environment. One must understand the essence of the nation's political heritage which still shapes and guides the conduct of government today as well as the physical, human, cultural and behavioral, social, economic, and international factors with which that government must work. These are the sources both of current national strengths and of weaknesses, the available facilitators of development (and hence of defense) as well as the obstacles to it. It is government's task to identify those societal factors conducive to development and then to maximize their utilization, while either eliminating or minimizing the negative impact of weaknesses and inadequacies.[1]

[1] A summary of major ecological factors and analysis of manpower characteristics is incorporated in Daniel Wit's study of Thai labor conditions. See *Labor Law and Practice in Thailand* (Washington, D.C.: U.S. Department of Labor, Bureau of Labor Statistics Report No. 267, March 1964), Part I, pp. 1–28.

20

The Thai Political Heritage

The political history of Thailand [2] reveals four fundamental characteristics of major importance in any assessment of the polity's role in society: (1) The polity has long been deeply rooted in the national culture (not alien to it) and thus has benefited from a significant degree of general consensus; (2) concurrently, it has been harmoniously and effectively interrelated with the social and economic structural-functional systems of society rather than clashing with them; (3) the interrelationships among the several strategic structural-functional systems have been such that the polity always has been overwhelmingly dominant while the other vital organizing systems have been ancillary to and supportive of it; (4) this historic pattern has continued down to the present despite various changes and modifications within the polity itself, changes which, of course, inevitably have been reflected in the other key systems too.

Within this centuries' old pattern of general consensus and political preeminence, a number of major political traditions have emerged as characteristically "Thai." They can be seen, despite periodic modifications and changes in the Thai state, almost from the time of the ancient Nanchao kingdom in South China to the present day. In broad outline, these traditions may be summarized as follows: (1) the dominance in society of relatively benevolent but authoritarian governmental leadership; (2) the periodic modernization of governmental structures (chiefly in response to external politico-military threats to national security) upon the basis of selective borrowings and adaptations from foreign societies; (3) the bureaucratization of politics; (4) the high degree of popular compliance with the decisions of government despite the absence of significant direct means for participation in the national political process.

[2] For extensive political analysis, see also David Wilson, *Politics in Thailand* (Ithaca, N.Y.: Cornell University Press, 1962).

The four Thai political traditions noted above have been manifested throughout the national history in varying ways. The oldest recorded Thai state—the kingdom of Nanchao in South China—was completely destroyed in 1253 by Kublai Khan's Mongols after some 300 years of successful resistance to Chinese imperial assaults and several hundred additional years of vassalage to the Chinese empire. In response to the overwhelming thirteenth-century Mongol onslaught, the Thai engaged in a mass migration into Southeast Asia and created a new kingdom based upon the capture of the Khmer (ancient Cambodian) imperial garrison at Sukhothai in what is now north-central Thailand. In the resultant Sukhothai kingdom (ca. 1238–1350), both state sovereignty and actual supreme political authority were concentrated in an absolute king whose ability to employ that power as he saw fit was characteristic of the entire period between 1238 and 1932. Initially, in the Sukhothai era, the monarch's role as Chief of State was heavily paternalistic and was viewed as comparable to that of the father of a family. In this capacity, the kings had direct contact with their subjects, particularly where petitions for redress of grievances or other claims for justice were made. They also served personally both as military commanders-in-chief and as heads of governments.

In exercising this generally benevolent authoritarianism, the Sukhothai rulers were at the pinnacle of a feudal-type system of territorial administration and socio-economic organization in which the various provinces were governed by loyal semihereditary nobles who, in turn, received the allegiance of warrior nobles operating from agricultural estates to which the peasantry was attached. Social and economic systems were integrated with the political system, whose domination was justified pragmatically by the ability of its hierarchy of royal and noble leaders to perform successfully such basic functions as the maintenance of law and order, the administration of justice, and the provision of military defense.

The Sukhothai kingdom began to disintegrate after the death

of its fourth monarch, Rama the Great. The fall of the kingdom led to its conquest by a lesser Thai principality, Utong.

Subsequently, the capital was moved to Ayudhya and a major modernization and expansion of the kingdom was undertaken by the new ruler, King Rama Tibodi I. Under the new Ayudhyan regime, impressive transformations in political, administrative, and socio-economic structures were introduced to meet the governmental requirements of a greatly expanded state. The conquest of the Indianized and neighboring Khmer empire greatly enlarged the Thai state. Consequently, the initial preeminence of governmental leadership, anchored to the kingship role, was elaborated and greatly expanded. The justification for monarchical absolutism was extended far beyond the "father of the people" concept to incorporate the Hindu Brahman belief in royal semi-divinity. Under this revision, whose essence was brought to Thailand mainly by the conquered Khmer elites as part of their Indian heritage and governmental experience, the occupant of the throne became a "Buddha-to-be." He was made into a demigod surrounded by elaborate ceremony, no longer easily accessible to his subjects, and the object of total obedience because of his religious as well as his administrative and military chieftainship. Limited only by the ethical necessity to behave righteously, and with authority enhanced by the view that all others in the kingdom were his servants and personal property, the Ayudhyan king became the most absolute of rulers, the possessor of both religious and secular authority.

This massive accretion of the king's personal authority was made operational, in theory, through a comparable enhancement of his government's actual power over all sectors of the society. The Khmerization of the kingdom had resulted both from the very pragmatic need of the kings to increase their governmental capabilities to deal with the considerably expanded Thai realm, and from the intellectual and cultural influence exercised over them by the enslaved Cambodian elites (an influence similar to that of the

Greeks over their Roman masters). Ayudhya, therefore, also incorporated and adapted into its system many Khmer administrative practices which had been developed to rule the latter's once great empire. The result was the development of a Thai bureaucratic elite in charge of a much more centralized administrative machine as well as, in effect, the bureaucratization of the entire population. For the nobles and warriors, who previously had governed the provinces and subdistricts as lords bound in a feudal relationship to the king, were transformed into government officials and were deprived of their earlier semiautonomous territorial power bases. The peasants, for their part, were freed from the land and were bound directly to the king for purposes of allegiance, taxes, and other required services. However, they were placed under the administrative supervision of the functionally relevant royal officials.

As part of this new centralization and modernization of government, the public administrative structures also were given increased functional specialization to meet the requirements of a larger and more complex kingdom. Thus, all central administration was placed in either a civil or a military division, each of which was divided into departments headed by ministers and entrusted with both functional and territorial responsibilities. The first four of these departments were Treasury, Agriculture, Royal Household (both palace affairs and judicial activities), and Interior.[3]

To maximize both royal power and societal integration, moreover, every adult male in Ayudhya was ranked (see p. 69) and thereby incorporated into a national hierarchy headed by the king. However, official titles and positions were not inherited; persons assumed as names the titles attached to their positions (and changed titles when they changed positions); and all inherited wealth was divided equally among the sons of a family. As a result,

[3] For a summary of Thai administrative history, see M. Ladd Thomas, "Thai Public Administration," *The New Zealand Journal of Public Administration*, XXV, No. 1 (September 1961), 10–14.

the Ayudhyan kingdom functioned through an absolute and semi-divine king, aided by a "nameless" bureaucracy (the Thai obtained family names only in the twentieth century) which was devoid of job security or an independent power base, and was inserted into an elaborate, flexible, national hierarchy of superior-subordinate relationships.

Under this system, not only was the feudal aristocracy emasculated but both the economy and the social structure were even more completely interrelated as adjuncts of royal absolutism and its dependent bureaucracy. In the absence of commercial and industrial revolutions such as those which produced middle classes in post-feudal Europe, the agrarian Thai kingdom thus became one of the most absolutist and statist in the pre-totalitarian world. Although the kingdom was never sufficiently modern and industrialized to warrant characterization as totalitarian, social status, economic power, advanced education, and official position were all inextricably intertwined. The only significant avenue to the first three lay through membership in the official bureaucracy. All leaders of the society and its various subsystems were government officials, and no independent socio-economic leadership capable of challenging this domination of government ever emerged.

During its 400 years, therefore, the Ayudhyan kingdom expanded and deepened the Thai tradition of authoritarian government as well as such behavioral traits as the submissiveness of inferiors to superiors, mass willingness to accept with little question the decision-making authority of governmental superiors, and general popular political apathy. The basis for governmental decisions was not questioned because it was assumed that the decision-makers were morally virtuous. As a result, no subsequent regime down to the present day either has been able to or has desired to ignore this heritage. The Thai masses, for their part, have never yet indicated any strong, deeply rooted, or widespread insistence either that their leadership be democratized or that there be a fundamental transformation in the structuring of their society.

Ayudhya was destroyed by the Burmese in 1767, after a series of wars which spread over two centuries. Once again, however, the Thai people demonstrated their historic vitality and recuperative powers by creating another kingdom, this time based in Bangkok. The new Chakri dynasty rallied the people and reorganized the state. After successfully containing and then driving back the Burmese, its kings subsequently were confronted by an Anglo-French colonialism which was engulfing all the other states of Southeast Asia. In the face of this new imperialist threat, the Chakri kings decided that Thai national independence could not be maintained just by efforts to insulate or to isolate the kingdom. Rather, a diplomacy which sought to establish a regional balance of power by playing off the two Western empires had to be combined with territorial and commercial concessions plus an internal modernization program which deprived them of any justification for direct intervention in Thai affairs. As a result, from 1851—when Rama IV (King Mongkut) assumed the throne—to 1932 —when a coup d'etat limited the power of Rama VII—the Thai provided further evidence of that selective cultural flexibility and assimilative capacity which had enabled ancient Nanchao to borrow from China, and the Sukhothai and Ayudhyan kingdoms to draw upon the more developed Indian and Khmer civilizations. Nevertheless, even the significant governmental and administrative reforms of this era, some of which ultimately led to the 1932 overthrow of royal absolutism, did not reorder the basic nature of the polity's role in society or its relations with the economy and the social system.

Turning to the West for inspiration, since it now was the most powerful external force, post-1850 Siam sought to avoid any charge that the kingdom was a barbaric state incapable of and unwilling to protect foreigners or otherwise to adhere to modern international standards of law and justice. Rama IV (King Mongkut) and Rama V (King Chulalongkorn), therefore, further modified the role of kingship; increased the degree of specialization and centralization of governmental structures along Western lines; established a civil service system, training program, and fixed salary scale for government personnel; introduced a Western concept of citizenship which replaced both slavery and the previous lack of popular legal rights against the throne; began the creation of modern transportation and communications systems; promoted the limited creation of factories; and entered into extensive commercial relations with the West which necessitated major changes in legal, judicial, and economic practices.

Such limited and selective westernization during the last half of the nineteenth century was followed during the first three decades of the twentieth century by the establishment under Rama VI (1910–1925) of compulsory public education (1921) and the promotion of a new Thai nationalism. Rama VII (1925–1935), for his part, although apparently desiring to cap the political modernization process with constitutional monarchy, inadvertently helped to produce a less satisfactory development. Because of his heavy dependence upon the advice of an aristocratic oligarchy which had acquired dominance in the state and society during his reign, he failed to take the necessary actions to establish the British-type monarchy he visualized. The result was the 1932 coup d'etat and the militarized, oligarchical regime which presently exists.

In the case of the monarch's role, the definition which had operated under the Chakri kings until 1932 had modified and blended both the Sukhothai conception of the king as paternalistic "father of the people" and the majestic mysticism and ceremonial which had surrounded the Ayudhyan sovereigns. Without lessening the absolute character of kingship, first Rama IV and then Rama V de-emphasized the use of divine right as an exclusive basis for royal preeminence and eliminated many of the practices which had prostrated (literally and figuratively) the entire populace before a semidivine ruler. Instead, the king became an exalted chief whose justification for leadership was founded both on heredity and on his ability, pragmatically, to perform the essential functions of government effectively and with justice. While refusing to acknowledge "any rule, thing, or persons" capable of limiting royal power, Rama V was, in effect, saying, "in truth any act of the king must be appropriate and just." Kingship, therefore, was somewhat humanized and rationalized, being reassociated with an acknowledged sense of responsibility to all classes of the people and partially removed from the earlier aura of mysticism which had provided it with limitless theoretical power but decreasing amounts of actual effective control over government. Royal absolutism was more clearly focused, linked to supreme operational authority, and subjected to potential evaluation in terms of the administrative competence with which the role was performed. A new determinant of loyalty to government thus was introduced, in addition to the traditional ones.

Related to the changes in the role of the monarch under the Chakri kings, Thai governmental structures and practices were consciously westernized from 1850 to 1932 in order to enhance their performance efficiency. Rama IV thus introduced the practice of employing European advisors, each drawn from a different country, in order to maintain a balance of foreign influence among them while obtaining the desired assistance in improving his administration. *Corvée* labor was also replaced on state projects by paid labor, wherever possible. Rama IV's great son, Rama V, replaced the traditional Ayudhyan departments of government with more functionally specialized Western-type ministries in the fields of Foreign Affairs, Defense, Interior, Justice, Finance, Education, Agriculture, Public Works, Royal Household, Royal Services, and the Capital. Moreover, the large degree of autonomy which had come to characterize the previous ministries was reduced, ministerial budgets and a system of accounting to the king for expenditures was required, tax collection was improved, and the king's personal funds were distinguished from those of the state. By 1892, this reorganization of central administration also led to the establishment of a Council of Ministers, which met regularly under the king's chairmanship and served as an advisory cabinet. It also produced a Council of State, composed of princes and noblemen, which was accorded advisory legislative power, plus a Privy Council, which was designed to brief the king as preparation for his discussions with the Council of State.

Other major governmental reforms of the period included the creation of a royal pages' school to train future officials, the sending of selected sons—first of the aristocracy and later of the commoner elite—to European schools, and the reform of provincial and local administration in order to centralize it under the Minister of Interior as well as to regularize and professionalize its conduct. Universal military conscription was established, too, in order to regularize military service in defense of the country.

The nineteenth-century modernization efforts of Ramas IV and V, launched because they recognized that the country's very survival depended in large measure on such innovation, served to promote both national independence and the well-being of Thai society. As such, this outstanding display of leadership stood in marked contrast to that exercised either by neighboring Southeast Asian rulers during the same period or by that of the great Chinese empire to the north. Only Japan, in Asia, consciously took a similar course for similar reasons. Nevertheless, in launching this necessary process of governmental modernization, forces also were generated in Thailand which eventually replaced royal absolutism with the current authoritarianism of a militarized commoner-oligarchy.

For one thing, the traditional basis for royal absolutism was definitely weakened by the pre-1932 reduction in the monarch's claims to semidivinity, the royal assumption of personal responsibility for government, and the suggestion that supreme leadership was justifiable chiefly in terms of administrative competence and dedication to the nation's well-being. When this weakening was coupled with a modernization of governmental structures and their staffing, the foundation was laid for future demands by the increasingly professionalized bureaucratic elites to govern in their own right, particularly when less decisive and competent kings succeeded to the throne in the twentieth century. Moreover, the question of popular participation in the political system was bound ultimately to be raised since it was becoming a characteristic of the new age.

Simultaneously, the great governmental reforms of Ramas IV and V inevitably caused modification in the interrelationships of the political, social, and economic subsystems. By introducing the Western concept of citizenship and the yardstick of administrative competence in evaluating governmental personnel, the basis of loyalty to government was changed somewhat. With the further introduction of some modern transportation and communications, selected types of factory machinery, new fiscal and economic regulations, and westernized legal and judicial procedures, the development process inevitably conditioned the economic and social structures although its carefully controlled character avoided revolutionary changes. Contemporary Thailand, therefore, is still very much in the throes of adjustment to those modernization forces introduced into the society during the last half of the nineteenth century by two imaginative and innovative kings.

The period from 1910 (when Rama V died) to 1932 (when limited monarchy was imposed) constitutes a second stage in the Chakri-led modernization of the Thai state. During these years, the revised definition of kingship was maintained, as was the process of limited westernization. However, Rama VI (1910–1925), educated in England at both Sandhurst and Oxford, devoted himself less to the further transformation of governmental structures than he did to the problems of molding the Thai people into a modern and unified nation. His method was that of promoting nationalism, which he saw as a modern substitute for the more traditional and semifeudal oaths of allegiance which bound subjects to the regime under his predecessors. Moreover, he also felt that, with a new unity rooted in nationalism, the country would be better able to acquire complete equality in those late-nineteenth-century treaty relationships which the West had virtually imposed on Thailand. In his efforts to mold Thai political culture in this fashion, the King experimented with various organizations (e.g., a Wild Tiger Corps of citizens organized on a para-military basis), slogans ("religion, king, and nation"), and the launching of a campaign against the unassimilated resident Chinese. Despite the criticism to which many of these activities could be and were subjected, the basic thrust of Rama VI's reign continued the westernization of the Thai state.

Rama VII, who came to the throne in 1925 and abdicated in 1935, was destined to provide royal acquiescence in the termination of absolute monarchy and the entry by Thailand into a third phase of political development. Personally lacking the dynamism and forcefulness which had characterized in varying ways his three immediate royal predecessors, his reign was confronted from the outset by serious economic problems as well as by evidence of stirrings against the throne: There had been an abortive military coup in 1912 to compel acceptance of a constitutional monarchy and a contemplated one in 1917 directed against Rama VI's decision to enter World War I on the Allied side. Rama VII, therefore, sought assistance by urging the members of the various advisory royal councils established by Rama V, as well as of a new Supreme State Council which he had created, to speak freely. Moreover, he permitted the opinions of his aristocratic advisors to influence his decisions. The result of such liberalization of kingship, unfortunately, was the emergence of a relatively illiberal princely clique whose ability to influence the monarch was further enhanced by its members' monopolization of senior positions in the bureaucracy, both civil and military. Thus, although the King increasingly wrote and spoke of the necessity to culminate his country's political modernization and development with the establishment of a constitutional monarchy, he allowed himself to be dissuaded from providing the required leadership for such a change by the coterie of senior princes who surrounded him.

It was at this juncture in Thai history, when the traditional leadership failed to continue its previously assumed role of presiding over the modernization and development of the state and society, that a new elite emerged and seized control of the kingdom. Not surprisingly, this elite was composed primarily of Western-educated (chiefly in France) members of the bureaucratic commoner elite, civil and military. These Thai, with their European education and experience, were frustrated in their careers by the princely oligarchy which dominated government and society and by the new economy measures which had reduced government personnel rolls and salaries. In addition, they were the ideological beneficiaries both of that new nationalism which Rama VI had launched in Thailand and of their European experience with nationalism and constitutionalism. In the light of the deterioration of royal absolutism both in theory and in practice by 1932, and their loss of a sense of satisfaction with the benefits to be derived from the established order, these commoner bureaucrats staged a successful and relatively bloodless coup d'etat. The result was the proclamation of a limited monarchy and the transfer of real power from king and princes to a new commoner oligarchy. In the absence of European-type middle classes, it now fell to the Thai equivalent —the commoner senior bureaucrats—to lead the nation into the next stage of political development.

The basic characteristics of the Thai state since the 1932 coup demonstrate clearly the extent to which the regime is heir to the heritage outlined above. For, although royal absolutism has been replaced by limited monarchy and the occupants of the highest positions of power and authority are overwhelmingly drawn from a new source (the military and civil bureaucracy), present-day Thailand nevertheless is still largely a product of authoritarian government engaged in the management of a relatively pragmatic, careful, and conservative process of societal evolution. The traditional characteristics of old Siam have been partially adjusted to meet some of the demands of a new age, but they certainly have not been uprooted and discarded. Governmental leadership has continued to evidence a willingness to experiment cautiously with modernization and development, but only to an extent deemed necessary to meet major pressures and only in ways which, as much as possible, do not seriously upset the country's historic sources of stability: the traditional culture; traditional behavior patterns; and traditional relationships between government, the economy, and the social system.

As to new external threats to national security, the Japanese threat of the World War II era was handled by Thai diplomacy through a policy which provided administrative cooperation in exchange for the preservation of Thai authority over the state and society. Today, Chinese and North Vietnamese Communist threats to Thailand—even more than the earlier ones from Burma, Britain, France, and Japan—make further modernization and development a critical prerequisite to Thai national independence. For Thailand is endangered not merely in the traditional terms of possible open invasion but also in the new terms of revolutionary warfare waged from within the society. Thus, the Thai leadership must attend not only to its military bulwarks—with the aid and support of a great power, like the United States, which is capable of maintaining a balance of power in Southeast Asia—but also to any significant domestic problems which serve as sources of disruption and could be exploited for subversive purposes. Given the extent to which Communism in the underdeveloped lands makes its appeal primarily to the local would-be modernizers as well as to those with deep-seated grievances against the established order, this particular externally promoted pressure requires a response in the form of extensive renovation and broad-scale modernization of Thai economic, cultural, social, and political structures and behavior.[4]

Physical Environment

LOCATION

To a significant degree, the operative standards of value, the beliefs, sentiments, traditions, customs, and ideas of Thailand, as with all countries, are a result of human interactions within a

[4] For an analysis of Thai foreign policy and the Communist threat, see Donald E. Nuechterlein, *Thailand and the Struggle for Southeast Asia* (Ithaca, N.Y.: Cornell University Press, 1965).

specific physical environment. The present Thai kingdom is located in the center of the Southeast Asian peninsula. Its area of approximately 200,000 square miles (almost the size of France) comprises about one-third of the total peninsula, Thailand extending almost 1,000 miles from north to south and 500 miles from east to west. It is based on territory which the Thai have occupied for seven centuries. Anchored to the great and fertile Chao Phraya River Basin (71,081 square miles), which is its historic heartland, the early Thai kingdoms were able at times to expand north into the Burmese uplands and to the Chinese border, east across the Mekong River into what are now Laos and Cambodia, and south into the Malayan peninsula. That same location, however, also has made Thai territory easily accessible to neighboring foreign expansionism. On one basis or another, therefore, Thai society has always been extensively involved in that movement of peoples and of armed forces which has continuously characterized the entire peninsula's history.

As far as Thailand's current borders are concerned, to the north, on the other side of scattered mountain passes leading through the Himalayan foothills, lies the southwestern Chinese province of Yunnan. It is some 81 miles from the Thai frontier at its nearest point and is separated from it by only a narrow half-circle of territory, which the Burmese and Laotians share. Various hill tribes roam this mountainous area without regard to national boundaries or the security of the Thai state. Potentially, therefore, southwestern China is a springboard for invasion of Thailand just as, in the twelfth and thirteenth centuries, it was the starting point for the Thai migration into Southeast Asia.

To the north and east is contemporary Laos. Its long border with Thailand is formed chiefly by the Mekong River, which originates in Tibet and China, and is traversable for extended distances, cutting through a delta valley which also offers no serious physical obstacles to the flow of people. An expansionist regime on the east bank of the Mekong, therefore, is always a major threat to Thai security. The country, moreover, is accessible from Cambodia on the southeast—as the early Thai wars against the Khmers and modern conflicts with the French have demonstrated.

On the south, the Thai border with the Malay states of the past also provided no obstacle to military movements in both directions. Thus Thailand obtained its present four southern provinces, peopled chiefly with ethnic Malays, through a military expansion into the Malay peninsula that began in the thirteenth century and was contained within its present limits only after the World War II defeat of the Thai ally, Japan. More recently (1948–1960), Malayan Communist guerrillas (largely of Chinese ethnic origin) were able to rest and train on the Thai side of the border during their long but unsuccessful revolutionary war. Today, perhaps 500 hard-core guerrillas still inhabit that border area and have maintained a headquarters base against all efforts by both Thai and Malayan governments to eliminate them. As to Burma on the west, existing borders are a product of past wars with the Burmese (sixteenth-nineteenth centuries) and of a twentieth-century settlement with the British colonial government of Burma.

This overland accessibility of the Thai location, furthermore, is complemented by its sea front. There are some 1,200 miles of southern border arcing around the Gulf of Siam and linking the country to the lands to be reached across the China Sea. On the southwest, limited access to and from the Indian Ocean also exists. It is largely because of this combined land-sea accessibility of the Thai homeland that the country has been subjected to so many foreign threats during its long history of independence.

Thailand's historic geographical involvement with the outside world has helped to produce a number of the important attitudes and traditions of its contemporary political culture. Interacting with other sources of the national culture, to be discussed later, the Thai's many experiences with foreign threats to national security have contributed to (1) a basic sense of nationhood as well as a commitment to and pride in national independence (*Thai* means *free*); (2) a commitment to monarchy, which has constituted the historic political form through which the national existence has been promoted successfully for 700 years; (3) a tradition of strong political leadership capable of meeting and overcoming the periodic foreign challenges to national survival; (4) a tradition of willingness by the political leadership to engage in that degree of change and of modernization, particularly of government, necessary to preserve the kingdom's independence from foreign domination.

CLIMATE, TOPOGRAPHY, SOIL, AND AGRICULTURE

Climate, topography, the nature of the soil, and ancient Asian ways of producing food also have played a major part in molding Thai culture, behavior, and institutions. Since Thailand is located completely within the tropics and is part of monsoon Asia, it is swept alternately by the warm moist winds moving from the Indian Ocean toward central Asia to the north, as well as by the cooler and drier winds coming down from the Asian highlands on their way back to the ocean. This rhythmic pattern produces three distinct seasons: a rainy season, when the ocean winds deposit their heavy rainfall (late April or May to October); a cool season, when the Himalayan winds first begin their passage back to the ocean (about November to February); and a hot season, when the winds are still dry but the freshness has been lost (late February to about May).

During the rainy season, intermittent but regularly repeated heavy showers produce almost 90 percent of the rainfall received by the largest and most fertile area—the Central Plain and its Chao Phraya River Basin. Most of the rain in the more mountainous north as well as throughout the rest of the land is concentrated in this period. This rainfall is sufficiently great to provide the Central Plain with an annual average of 59 inches, the western windward slopes of the northern hills with as much as 120 inches, the Northeast with an annual average of about 30 inches, and the rest of the country with some 40 inches of rain. Temperatures during this same season range in the Central Plain from a mean maximum of 98 degrees to a mean minimum of about 80 degrees, with the mountainous North being somewhat cooler. Variations in

temperature between the rainy and hot seasons are minor, however, and only the brief cool season actually reduces the tropical heat to something approximating spring in the temperate zone of the world.

The special significance of this climatic pattern, apart from the impact of such hot weather on human vigor and the work day, derives from its relation to Thai agriculture and the pattern of living which has characterized the overwhelming majority of the population throughout history. For the traditional Thai life cycle has been shaped to a great extent by rice cultivation which, in turn, necessarily has been adjusted to the prevailing conditions of soil and of climate. In response to these factors the Thai people, forming one of the greatest rice-producing societies in the world, plant their rice at the beginning of the rainy season and, thereafter, traditionally rely primarily on the rains and resultant flooding of rivers and streams to produce the crop which is their society's economic foundation. Water rushes down from the northern highlands, which rim the country and serve as a great watershed. Not only the lowlanders but also the hill peoples take advantage of the season to begin the planting of their rice and maize; the latter burn brush and trees to create wet ashes in the clearings in which the planting is done. With this rainfall and the existence of large blocks of alluvial land, only the simplest of irrigation has been undertaken or proved necessary up to the present to produce an abundant rice crop. Subsistence, then, is relatively easy for most of the population, and this fact undoubtedly has negatively affected to some unmeasurable extent its achievement motivation.

Once the planting has taken place, the Thai farmers will fish in their streams, in the canals crisscrossing the Central Plain, and even in the flooded rice paddies, while some (particularly the women) may engage in simple cottage industries, and others temporarily will enter the unskilled urban labor force to earn cash for the purchase of various consumer goods and possibly more paddy. Harvesting of the crop occurs in the fall at the end of the rainy season and as the weather is turning cooler. Thus, the historic Thai commitment to rice cultivation, and the relation of that to climatic and soil conditions, has fostered a traditional cycle of sowing, harvesting, resting and sowing again, interwoven by various holidays and festivities which also, in large part, involve Buddhist blessings for the crops and animistic propitiation of spirits.

From this form of agricultural existence which, with the inclusion of fishing and forestry, still involves up to 85 percent of the population and is organized about small family-owned and -operated farms, the Thai have developed much of their view of the good life and many of their values and attitudes. The bountiful rice crop and other products of the soil, in combination with a lack of population pressure on the land (only 131 persons per square mile in 1960 as compared to Japan's 550), have given the Thai a standard of living which is significantly higher than that of most other Asians (roughly three times that of India, for example). Living in small agricultural villages, and with enough land so that no major agricultural worker groups have emerged, their way of life has contributed to the development of a large degree of individual, familial, and communal self-sufficiency as well as to a sense of individual dignity and of equality of opportunity. Most important is the fact that the Thai government traditionally has not interfered with this way of life other than to enhance it. For most Thai, then, life has appeared good and economic survival not very difficult. Even the Thai approach to Theravada Buddhism, the national religion, has been heavily colored by this simple but historically satisfying agricultural existence.

In this adaptation to their climate and land the Thai people have developed certain values, attitudes, and traditions which can be summarized, in general, as follows: (1) a belief that agriculture, and particularly rice cultivation, is the most worthwhile and ennobling form of labor; (2) conversely, an historic distaste for commercial activity and disinterest in permanent urban living; (3) a sense of self-reliance, personal dignity, and economic independence; (4) an agricultural sense of time and a behavioral discipline which is very different from that required by modern commercial and industrial pursuits; (5) a psychological and cultural sense of well-being, which has contributed to patterns of behavior which most foreigners customarily designate as "happy-go-lucky," "friendly," "easy-going," "party-going"; (6) a basic faith in the virtue of their way of life and country; (7) a basic political apathy, since few demands have had to be made on government other than for occasional protection and for simple local administrative facilitation of their pursuits; (8) an historic absence of popular revolt against government; (9) a basic societal stability—politically, economically, and socially; (10) a largely classless rural society which diverges sharply from the smaller but more stratified and commercial urban society.

NATURAL REGIONS AND RESOURCES

Thailand's greatest natural resource is its land, whose cultivation always has been, as just noted, the economic foundation of the society and a major conditioner of Thai life and behavior. The country consists of four distinct natural regions: the North (or Northwest), the Northeast (the Korat Plateau), the Central Plain (the Chao Phraya Basin), and the South (the isthmus leading to the Malayan peninsula). Among these regions, the Central Plain is the economic, social, cultural, and political heartland—the core area to which the country is anchored. It is 71,081 square miles in size (more than one-third of the total land area of Thailand), and extends about 120 miles north from the Gulf of Siam, forming a great alluvial plain bisected by the Chao Phraya River and crisscrossed by its tributaries as well as by innumerable canals. Its extremely rich soil, constituting about 50 percent of all cultivated land, is almost one continuous rice paddy in the midst of which resides approximately one-third of the nation's population. With relatively little effort and the employment of only the simplest of agricultural technology, this vast plain produces one of the largest rice crops in the world. In addition, its river banks sustain various fruit trees such as mango and are also cultivated to produce sugar cane, vegetables, and jute.

The some 60,000 square miles of the North are subdivided into deep alluvial valleys defined by long mountain ridges which run in a north-south direction. Drained by the tributaries of the Chao Phraya River, these valleys are rich and easily support substantial rice cultivation as well as cotton, soybeans, and peanuts. In addition, the mountain forests of the North are one of the world's great suppliers of teak, as well as ebony and rosewood, and lend themselves to such types of forest product industry as resins, gums, tree oils, lac, charcoal, firewood, pulpwood, etc. The mountain soil also has been able to produce a very good Virginia-type tobacco. Moreover, the North has some low-grade coal and lignite deposits, small oil reserves and wolfram deposits. More than one-quarter of the population resides in the region.

The South is also wealthy in natural resources. Its approximately 20,000 square miles, jutting out into the Indian Ocean, are relatively mountainous and contain only narrow valleys and a limited cultivable area along the eastern sea coast. Nevertheless, the forests have valuable timber resources; there are some coal deposits and very substantial tin reserves; and the coastal plain has been able to produce major quantities of rubber as well as of rice, coconut palms, sugar cane, and fruit. Approximately one-ninth of the population resides here.

In contrast to the other three regions, the Thai Northeast has been the country's economically depressed area. Constituting approximately one-third of the total land area (65,724 square miles), it is composed primarily of the Korat Plateau and those adjoining lands which run along the west bank of the Mekong River border with Laos. Vast sections of the region are desolate, other parts have sandy, poorly drained soil, and cultivation is further complicated by a very inadequate water supply and a short rainy season, unlike most of the rest of the country. This resource-poor area is inhabited by approximately one-third of the population.

Thailand's basically rich agricultural land, extensive forests, and substantial tin deposits are supplemented by very substantial fresh-water and marine fish resources. Moreover, although fuel resources are quite limited—low-grade coal deposits in the North and in the southwestern coastal highlands, lignite in the North and South, scattered oil shale resources and limited oil reserves in the Chao Phraya Basin and in the North—there is considerable hydroelectric potential provided by the upper tributaries of the Chao Phraya and Mekong Rivers. Apart from tin, there exist only limited mineral deposits—the major natural resource weakness of the country. However, even in this case, there are some reasonably high-grade iron ore deposits in the Central Plain which, although probably not sufficient to support any significant steel industry, are exportable.

Overall, therefore, Thailand is reasonably rich in a sufficient number of basic natural resources to sustain a substantial population on a level which, in traditional Asian terms, is fairly high. Only in the Northeast is there a naturally depressed area whose economic growth problems are very difficult to resolve. Unfortunately, however, that is also the region which has been targeted for Communist revolutionary warfare.

CHAPTER III

✿

The People and Their Society

The Human Resource

The vital catalyst in any country's development is always the human being, himself. It is therefore essential to identify the major prevailing characteristics of Thailand's human resources as well as those cultural, social, and economic factors which, in addition to the country's political heritage and physical location, condition the Thai people's behavior. We need to know who and what the Thai are in order to judge their current development potential and self-defense capabilities.

DEMOGRAPHY

According to the 1960 census, Thailand's population was estimated to be 26,257,916. It is now probably about thirty million. At present, this estimate produces a relatively low average density of approximately 131 persons per square mile, as compared to Japan's 550 or the Philippines' 205. Even in terms of the square cultivated mile, the figure is only about 550. There are, of course, heavy localized population concentrations such as the 630 persons per square cultivated mile in the Chao Phraya valley (which includes Bangkok) and 3,000 people per square cultivated mile in limited sections of the southeastern coastal strip. Nevertheless, in this essentially agricultural society, the overall density of rural population is about 30 persons per square mile in the North, 35 persons in the South, 40 in the Northeast, and 145 in the Central Plain. Thailand, therefore, is relatively underpopulated at present, and the pressure of people upon its substantial natural resource base is still limited. However, the fact that the population is expanding at a rate of about 3 percent per year (the Thai National Economic Development Board estimated the expansion in 1960 at 3.88 percent) obviously means that this pressure is mounting and will require alleviation by expansion of food supplies sufficient to meet both the increasing domestic requirement and the country's agricultural export needs.

The population is also distributed in urban-rural terms in such fashion that an estimated 85 percent resides in rural Thailand, with 75 percent of the total population classified as members of agricultural households. Regionally, 55 percent of the Central Plain's population is agricultural, 79 percent of both the North and the South, and 88 percent of the Northeast. The almost even balance of urban-rural population in the Central Plain suggests both its greater industrialization and reflects the fact that over 50 percent of the country's total urban population resides in the twin city, national capital complex formed by Bangkok-Thonburi. According to the 1960 census, however, there were only 3,273,865 people living in the country's 120 municipalities, and only 17 of these towns and cities (including Bangkok with 1,299,528 and Thonburi with 403,818) had more than 25,000 persons; the third largest municipality, Chiengmai (in the North), containing 65,736 people. Such statistics further document the rural nature of the country. Moreover, although urbanization has been increasing steadily (a 1954 survey of Bangkok revealed that 38 percent of its population had migrated to the capital within the preceding seven years), many Thai are only temporary residents of the urban centers who return to their traditional villages after accumulating cash to buy rice land. There is still no great urbanization trend to date, therefore.

The Thai people, almost equally divided between males and females, is also very youthful. This is undoubtedly due to the still low average life span of approximately 50, in contrast to Japanese and American averages which exceed 65 for males and 70 for females. The estimated median age is 20, with 43 percent of the population composed of children under 15 and the remainder almost equally divided between those from 15 to 29 and those who are 30 or more. Almost 70 percent is under 30 and almost 82 percent is under 40. Statistics such as these are suggestive of the health, sanitation, dietary, and housing problems which confront the nation.

HEALTH, SANITATION, DIET AND HOUSING

The vigor of a people obviously depends not only upon motivation but also upon its physical condition. In the case of Thailand, that condition generally is good in Southeast Asian terms although extremely inadequate when compared with that of the Japanese people or of the other more developed nations of the world. Thai health and sanitary conditions have been steadily improving as a result of efforts by the Thai government, international organizations such as the World Health Organization, and the American foreign aid and technical assistance program. This improvement is reflected in the birth and mortality statistics. Thus, from 1947 to 1960 the birth rate increased from 23.7 to 36.9 per 1,000, while the death rate was reduced from 13.4 to 8.9 per 1,000 and the infant mortality rate from 80 to 49 per 1,000, with maternal mortality rates also being significantly reduced. Similarly, United Nations life expectancy estimates suggest that, from 1929 to about 1964, the average male's life span of 31.6 and female's life span of 37.4 increased to 48.69 and 51.90 respectively. Undoubtedly, such improvement has been continuing as modern medical facilities have been expanded and a number of diseases controlled or almost eliminated (malaria, for example).

45

Modern medical science is brought to the Thai citizenry, according to the 1960 census, by some 1,712 first- and second-class (no degree) physicians of whom 1,222 are government employees. This produced, in 1963, an estimated ratio of one physician for every 8,000 people; far better than the estimated Indonesian average of one doctor per 60,000 persons, but considerably below the American average of one per 800 people. In such categories as dentists, pharmacists, optometrists, nurses, medical technicians, etc., the figures for Thailand also reveal the need for major increases in modern health services even though many other non-Western countries suffer from greater shortages than do the Thai. The same generalization can be made about hospital, clinic, and nursing facilities. In conformity with almost universal patterns, moreover, those modern medical services and facilities which do exist are heavily concentrated in the few major metropolitan areas (particularly Bangkok), thereby seriously enhancing the inadequacies and shortages which prevail in the rural areas.

The major diseases which affect the Thai people, apart from those which are normal even in the Western world, stem both from poor sanitation and unhygienic conditions and from dietary deficiencies. Thus, a leading cause of death has been diseases of maternity and infancy. Intestinal diseases caused by impure water, little or no modern sewage disposal, and poor sanitation also wrack the population. To these may be added a relatively high incidence of tuberculosis, yaws, venereal disease, leprosy, and rabies. Nutritional imbalances are reflected in a significant amount of beri-beri and goiter, and many segments of the populace also suffer from riboflavin and iron deficiencies. These dietary deterrents to physical vigor are not a result of mass starvation by any means, since there is a plentiful supply of rice, fish, and fruit and also significant production of vegetables, meats and poultry. However, most Thai live mainly on polished rice with only a limited supplementation with other protective foods. All dietary inadequacies and diseases, as well as other health and sanitation problems, are greatest in the North and Northeast.

The existing public health and sanitation problems are due not only to serious shortages in modern medical facilities and services, or to nutritional imbalances, but also to widespread lack of popular understanding of the scientific basis for these problems. Despite steady expansion of the educational system, the masses of Thai still turn primarily to spirit exorcism and traditional herbs for medical relief. Even in public health campaigns to fight rabies, the authorities have faced cultural obstacles to the extermination of rabid dogs and other animals because of the Theravada Buddhist reluctance to destroy life. Nevertheless, the Thai people have been demonstrating a willingness to switch to modern medicines and to take various inoculations when their traditional remedies fail and modern health services are available to them. With improved understanding of medical science, this receptivity undoubtedly will increase.

Housing conditions in Thailand reflect both the simple agrarian character of life for most people and the tropical, monsoon climate. Rural homes are constructed of thatch, timber, and bamboo, and normally are built on stilts in order to provide shelter for the animals underneath as well as protection from the monsoon flooding. Urban workers customarily live in wood huts which frequently have tin sidings and thatch roofs. Upper income families, of course, have more elaborate housing in both rural and urban areas, with concrete and teak as well as other timber often making their homes, particularly in the case of urban elites, very splendid and westernized. Apart from the more elaborate urban homes, plumbing is still rare, and its absence further complicates the public health and sanitation problems of the country.

EDUCATION AND TRAINING

One of the most recent, systematic, and extensive discussions of human resource development and its problems has classified Thailand, on the basis of a statistical analysis of international educational data, as being at the bottom of the "semiadvanced" countries of the world in this respect. It is placed immediately above

Mexico and immediately below India in a list of 75 countries, thereby ranking it 36th from the top.[1] In this analysis, Thailand, like Mexico and India, is "barely self-sufficient in high level manpower resources . . ." and much closer in almost all respects to the "partially developed" list of countries immediately below it than to the top of the "semiadvanced" group, let alone to the nations classified as being "advanced" in their human resource development. This classification results from a composite index arrived at through an arithmetic totaling of enrollments in secondary education as a percentage of the age group 15 through 19 (adjusted for length of schooling) and of enrollments at the third or higher level of education as a percentage of the age group 20 through 24 (multiplied by a weight of 5 to take account of the greater importance to national development of this level). Based upon a recognition of the relationship between advanced formal education and high-level manpower, the study also documents, statistically, the high correlation between economic development and this form of human resource development.

Quantitatively, therefore, the semiadvanced nature of the Thai formal educational system is a major reason for, as well as a reflection of, the similarly intermediate level of its economic development. The 1960 census revealed that, out of a total of 21,147,582 people six years of age or older, 7,973,446 had no formal education. It also indicated that 7,370,600 had achieved the fourth grade in primary school or its equivalent; 276,272, the sixth grade of secondary school; 53,164, the second year of pre-university study; 95,137, some level of higher education; and 3,563, a graduate degree, including doctor of medicine.

The Thai educational system is underpinned by a compulsory primary education law enacted in 1921 as well as by the fact that government expenditures for educational services are now second only to expenditures for all forms of economic services. One im-

---

[1] Frederick Harbison and Charles A. Myers, *Education, Manpower and Economic Growth* (New York: McGraw-Hill, 1964); see p. 33 for table and pp. 23–48 for the general analysis.

portant result of the compulsory education law has been that, even though many rural children still do not attend school regularly, about 75 percent of all primary-age children are enrolled.

Because of this governmental concern for education, Thailand has achieved one of the highest literacy rates in Asia, the 1960 census indicating that 70 percent of the population 10 years of age or older can read and write in some language. However, the primary education provided has been designed chiefly to produce literacy plus some basic familiarity with Thai culture. Moreover, the system is hampered by the fact that classroom shortages make it necessary to hold approximately one-half of the primary schools in local Buddhist temples. Moreover, there are both severe teacher shortages and serious inadequacies in the preparation of existing teachers. A 1954 study, for example, estimated that as many as two-thirds of the primary school teachers did not then possess the required qualifications and that the recruitment of quality personnel was greatly hampered by low salaries. Although the situation has improved markedly during the last ten years with American assistance and increases in Thai expenditures for education, there remains much room for continued improvement in both quantitative and qualitative terms, if the Thai people are to be prepared for a more modern existence.

Secondary education in Thailand is organized into standard academic and vocational systems. Before completing the four and often five years (there frequently is a preliminary first year to learn the rudiments of reading and writing) of primary school and the passing of Ministry of Education examinations at the end of each year, students who are to continue divide into two groups. Those who pass the required competitive examinations for further academic study (and thereby for preparation leading to university admission) become eligible for standard secondary school. The others enter vocational training. The two groups combined represent about 30 percent of those who actually graduate from primary school.

The standard secondary school program builds upon that conducted in primary school but introduces the study of a foreign language; English is prescribed but generally is not spoken well by those who have studied it. If students desire to proceed to the university level, they take a two-year university preparatory course after completion of the six regular grades of secondary education. Examinations by the Ministry of Education must be passed, however, after completion of the third and sixth years of secondary study in order to continue, and there is a special examination prior to actual university matriculation. Estimates in 1961 indicated that, of the 70,000 students who graduated from the standard secondary schools, only 10,000 to 15,000 actually entered a university or equivalent program of study.

The vocational education system, administered by a Department of Vocational Education, is itself organized into three levels. Students may proceed through all three levels or transfer from a standard secondary school into one of the more advanced vocational schools. At the first level (comparable to grades eight to ten of standard secondary school), a three-year curriculum is provided in automechanics, metalwork, small-boat construction, tailoring, weaving, home economics, carpentry, building construction and masonry, enameling, and handicrafts. In 1961, about 18,000 students were enrolled. At the second level of vocational school (comparable to secondary academic grades eleven to thirteen), there is a three-year curriculum in modern languages, secretarial and commercial training, building and carpentry, welding and metallurgy, automechanics, telecommunications, machine shop, electrical and engineering trades, dressmaking, and women's crafts. About 30,100 students were studying at this level in 1961.

The most advanced vocational studies are concentrated in five multivocational technical institutes. These operate at the equivalent of a junior college level and give courses of three or more years in length, building upon the subject matter of the lower levels and introducing such subjects as electrical engineering, accountancy, architecture, business administration, and various skilled industrial trades. About 6,200 students were participating in 1961, bringing the total number of students for all 196 vocational schools to about 54,300. In addition, Thailand operates various teacher-training schools and colleges which in 1961 contained almost 20,000 students; the Thai Armed Forces and some civilian ministries have their own technological training programs; and there are a number of foreign-sponsored vocational programs (American, Australian, West German, and Japanese).

Thailand, therefore, does have a technological and vocational educational system which, with American assistance, has been improving steadily. Obviously, the numbers of students involved to date clearly suggest that the supply of persons with modern vocational and technological skills is extremely limited. At the same time, however, it is also worthwhile to take note of reports that the graduates of these schools and institutes sometimes have difficulty in obtaining appropriate jobs despite the great shortages of skilled manpower. Such difficulty stems from two types of problems: one technological and the other, cultural and behavioral. For, in many instances, the very modernity of the skills and training produces a situation in which the graduate cannot easily find shops or factories in his region which have the equipment that he has been trained to operate. On other occasions, he confronts the fact that Thai and Chinese businessmen often continue to emphasize apprenticeship learning over formal technical education, or else operate family enterprises in which all jobs of importance are reserved for relatives. Such obstacles to the effective utilization of even the very small Thai pool of technologically skilled persons are particularly great outside Bangkok. They also serve to document the very limited degree of economic modernization which characterizes the country as a whole. Clearly, there must not only be an expansion in the number of skilled workers but an expansion in the number of jobs which require skilled workers if economic progress is to be made.

University-level education in Thailand has been organized primarily around five universities and a College of Education—all located in Bangkok—plus several new regional universities currently being established. In addition, there are two Buddhist universities and several institutions of higher education operated by the Armed Forces. These institutions tend to specialize, with only two approaching broad academic coverage. Both faculty and students are often part-time. In 1961, the total enrollment for the six major institutions (and students regularly are carried on the rolls even though not actually taking courses for long periods of time) was 43,637, with 2,692 teachers. There were also about 4,000 Thai studying in foreign colleges and universities.

From the perspective of development, Thai higher education at both the secondary and university levels is characterized by its emphasis on studies designed to prepare students for careers in government or for general administrative responsibilities. University students, in particular, come mainly from the society's elites, and increasing numbers of qualified high school graduates are unable to enter because of shortages of facilities and faculty. Relatively few secondary and university students study scientific, technical, or managerial subjects, with resultant severe shortages in all types of modern high-level manpower. On the other hand, the fact that university and academic secondary school graduates are absorbed into the public service and the upper levels of the society has meant that the country has not faced the problems presented by the existence of a large, unemployed but educated group. To date, therefore, the Thai educational system has been in balance with the society's capacity to absorb its graduates. The absence of any significant number of idle, restless, and frustrated students has been a major factor in national stability. However, the Thai educational system has not been producing sufficient numbers of people with the skills and motivation required for major and rapid development. With educational opportunities expanding and economic modernization slowly occurring, a new balance of educational supply and demand at a more modern level increasingly will be necessary both to perpetuate societal stability and to promote national well-being.

MANPOWER RESOURCES

The economically active component of the Thai population, in 1960 census terms, was slightly more than 52 percent of the total population, with only 28 percent being 40 years of age or more. Since 85 percent of the people reside in rural areas, it is not surprising that 11,332,489 persons (82.3% of the work force), out of a total work force of 13,772,104, were classified as farmers, fishermen, hunters, and loggers. In contrast, there were only 173,960 professional and technical employees (1.3%) and 26,191 administrative, executive, and managerial employees (.2%). Craftsmen, production process workers, and related laborers were 806,205 (5.9%) of the total, with transport and communications workers numbering another 144,610 (1%). Clerical, sales, service, sport, and recreation workers totaled 1,163,135 (8.4%). Some 250,000 males were estimated to be in the Buddhist clergy on at least a temporary basis.

These and other basic manpower statistics reveal a number of developmentally significant characteristics. First, the nonagricultural sector is extremely small and involves only about 17 percent of the total work force. Second, within the nonagricultural sector, only about 8.5 percent of the work force is involved to any extent in industrial-type activity with, roughly, an equal percentage engaged in service, recreation, sales, or clerical work. Third, the Thai government itself probably employs about one-third of all nonagricultural wage earners, most of the industrial work force (in public enterprises), more than two-thirds of the professional and technical employees, and almost one-fourth of the handful of administrative, executive, and managerial employees (see p. 129). Fourth, the number of self-employed constitutes almost one-third of the total work force (agricultural and nonagricultural combined) and, when unpaid family workers are added to the self-employed, their number, then, comprises 12,111,228 Thai of the total work force of 13,772,104. Fifth, a very small percentage of

Thai have modern economic skills and are involved in modern economic activities.

Still other facts of importance about manpower are these: that a high percentage of the small number of agricultural wage earners (about 500,000 in all) are Thai-Lao whose poor land in the Northeast compels them to serve as migratory workers; that the limited number of Thai factories are engaged mainly in the production of light consumer goods; that the nonagricultural labor force includes large numbers of women and children (many performing heavy manual labor such as road building and construction); that many wage earners are just seasonal workers who serve in nonagricultural jobs only between planting and harvesting or for other short periods and, as a result, a major proportion of the nonagricultural work force (unskilled labor) also is basically rural in values and attitudes and uncommitted to urban life.

Thailand, therefore, is a country composed chiefly of self-employed farmers, fishermen, and forest workers who practice their occupations in relatively traditional fashion. There is still very little industrialization and only a relatively few people are engaged in nonagricultural activity. The result is a great shortage of skilled and semiskilled labor (most that exists is also Chinese rather than Thai) and an even greater shortage of managerial and high-level manpower. To modernize the Thai labor force, then, requires a major educational and training effort in combination with a significant transformation in traditional occupational preferences (agricultural or governmental), and in behavioral values and attitudes. Moreover, it also requires a significant increase in modern, nonagricultural employment opportunities for those who acquire the new skills.

Cultural and Behavioral Factors

Since the making of a modern man is essential to the entire process of modernization and development, and since modern man is characterized not only by his skills but also by his behavior, it is necessary to survey a people's cultural and behavioral characteristics in order to determine the extent to which they facilitate or deter modernization. Even though crude, such an inventory is essential to the subsequent formulation of the cultural component in any really adequate national development strategy.

Thai culture and behavioral characteristics are an historic distillation of centuries of continuous interaction between the people of the society, the physical location and environment of the homeland, foreign pressures and influences, and the several structural systems developed as responses to overriding societal needs. Despite various epic events in the country's political history (e.g., the thirteenth-century destruction of the Nanchao kingdom in China's Yunnan province by Kublai Khan's Mongols, subsequent mass migration from South China into Southeast Asia, fourteenth-century collapse of the Sukhothai kingdom, eighteenth-century destruction of the succeeding Ayudhyan kingdom by the Burmese, 1932 overthrow of the absolute monarchy, and, in World War II, Japanese military occupation), the nation's distinct culture has never been seriously ruptured. No complete and historic break with the past has really occurred. Instead, contemporary Thailand is heir to a relatively continuous cultural and political tradition which, although modified and adapted to changing circumstances at various times, has perpetuated and even reinforced certain outstanding behavioral characteristics through the centuries. Apart from values and attitudes reflective of environmental factors already discussed, the core of that culture is a complex of ethical, religious, and supernatural beliefs.

ETHICAL, RELIGIOUS, AND SUPERNATURAL BELIEFS

For an overwhelmingly agricultural society, most of whose members continue to follow a pattern of living which is very close to the centuries-old one, the traditional ethical-religious belief system remains a vital element of contemporary culture and behavior just as the historic church is, itself, a key institution. With mass immersion in modern communication still very limited and heavy reliance still placed on face-to-face contact, the infiltration and dilution of that belief system by Western culture has been restricted mainly to a minority of the population resident primarily in Bangkok. Moreover, even these urbanites follow behavior patterns which, although reflecting the impact of the West, nevertheless also remain very much "Thai."

In broadest terms, the Thai ethical-religious belief system is a composite of several separately identifiable but behaviorally intertwined strands, chief among which are Theravada Buddhism (which originated in ancient India), animism (which is rooted in the Thai contact with nature and the traditional rural existence), and pseudo-science (which blends certain beliefs in magic with certain systematic explanations of natural phenomena).

Theravada (Hinayana) Buddhism, as the most elaborate and philosophically best-formulated of the components of the ethical-religious belief system, is a particularly critical factor. Buddhism was brought to the Thai of Southwest China several centuries before their great twelfth- and thirteenth-century migrations into Southeast Asia. Today, approximately 94 percent of the entire population of Thailand is Buddhist, although the Chinese and Vietnamese minorities have their own amalgam of Mahayana Buddhism (the "northern" branch of the religion), Confucianism, and Taoism, while the Thai adhere to the "southern" branch of the religion. Theravada Buddhism also is the official religion of the royal family and the Thai state.

The religion, which its followers claim to be closest to the Buddha's original teachings is, in its undiluted formulation, a nonauthoritarian and nondogmatic philosophical inquiry into the truths which characterize the universe and man's role in it. Emphasizing the individual pursuit of salvation through the attainment of ethical enlightenment, it provides behavioral guides for "right action" which stress the importance of nonviolence, moderation rather than licentiousness, charity, and self-control—virtuous actions which will, it is believed, eliminate greed and envy (which are held to be the cause of man's suffering and ills). Such virtuous actions, as popularly understood by Theravada Buddhists, produce "merit"; and it is the process of increasing one's merit which offers the possibility of delivery from the cycle of birth, death, and reincarnation (the "wheel of life") and ultimate attainment of salvation in the sublime state of Nirvana (as close as Buddhists come to a concept of "heaven"). Although the process of seeking Nirvana unfolds through successive reincarnations, there is no guarantee that each new reincarnation will produce a better life for an individual. For Theravada Buddhism also includes the fundamental belief that while right action begets merit, and hence ensures improvement in one's condition in a future life, evil action generates evil results. Thus, man's happiness, well-being, status, and general condition in any given existence are determined by his personal ethical behavior in a previous existence.

This Theravada Buddhist form of individualism is distinctly different from that which has emerged in the West, particularly since the Reformation. It is associated with a belief in the virtue of noninvolvement in the struggles of society. Man's physical labor or the application of human intelligence to the solution of worldly problems is not eulogized or even considered to be the means to a better life. Rather, the existing condition, both good and bad, of all humans is regarded as the just reward for previous virtue or lack thereof. There is, then, in Theravada, no clarion call for social, economic, or political action either to improve an individual's personal condition or to right the world's wrongs. As a result, Theravada Buddhism (in contrast to the new political activities of Mahayana Buddhists in South Vietnam or in Ceylon) tends to be socially passive. Its individualism is one of self-knowledge and self-control, with each person bearing the responsibility for his own condition in life as a result of his degree of adherence to Buddhist morality. The "don'ts" of life—don't defraud, commit adultery, deceive, kill, or otherwise practice greed and envy—are indicated, but positive action of a worldly character to aid either oneself or one's fellow humans is not proclaimed. Certain individual acts of charity and of benevolence are suggested, but there is no philosophical or religious justification for human struggle to change the world.[2] Instead, there is a tendency to regard such efforts to dominate environment as almost blind presumption and the height of egotism (hence, moral weakness). It is believed that the basic laws governing the universe are immutable and that the key to successful comprehension and compliance with them is philosophic, involving actions of morality rather than of materialism.

From this very cursory outline of that part of Theravada Buddhism which is pertinent to an analysis of Thai social behavior, one can deduce the following contributions from it to the nation's culture: (1) There is an emphasis on the autonomy of all men, upon their individual rather than their collective pursuit of a better life, with the ultimate goal being one of complete escape from the cares of the world. (2) There is an emphasis on ethical behavior, particularly the negative aspects of such behavior (the "don'ts"), as the means of pursuing personal improvement—morally as well as materially. Neither individual nor collective economic, social, or political action is suggested as the appropriate means of improving man's lot. Efforts to develop society or its subsystems are not implied. (3) Justification is provided for passivity in the face of personal and certainly collective distress since the conditions of life, both individual and collective, are a direct result of the type of morality practiced by individuals in a previous existence. (4) Justification for submission to authority is provided and respect for those whose condition in life is better since their positions presumably have been earned by the attainment of moral merit. (5) The religion, while stressing the equal opportunity of all men to improve their condition and even to attain Nirvana, provides a moral basis for hierarchy. (6) The religion also has constituted an ethical restraint upon the holders of positions of power and authority, and probably has limited tensions between rulers and

[2] See Paul Tillich, *Christianity and the Encounter of the World's Religions* (New York: Columbia University Press, 1963), pp. 53–75.

ruled by encouraging acquiescence on the part of the latter and benevolence on the part of the former.

In sum, despite the many ethically attractive values imbedded in Theravada Buddhism—its emphasis on human moral equality and on personal moral behavior, the assistance provided man in meeting distress with a measure of equanimity, the stress on self-reliance and responsibility for one's actions, etc.—and despite the religion's contribution to societal stability and the moderation of political absolutism, it does not provide a religious basis for positive action either to achieve societal development or political democracy. However, it also does not constitute an absolute barrier to such social action, and it does permit development of the sort which occurred in the West as the latter moved from medievalism and feudalism into the making of the modern Western world.

Interwoven with Theravada Buddhism in the Thai ethical-religious system is an animism whose roots are pre-Buddhist and whose beliefs and practices are distinctly outside the framework of precepts propounded by the Buddha. Nevertheless, animistic practices constitute an important part of Thai behavior, being most significant in the case of the masses of the society and least among the urban educated and intellectual groups, many of whom are adherents of a religious reform (neo-Buddhism) which would strip away many of the popular encrustations on and modifications of the basic principles of the religion.

The attitudes created by Thai animistic beliefs are fairly simple, although compelling. For the most part, these beliefs derive from the view that the universe is inhabited by a variety of spirits who dominate the course of events. With this in mind, it has become customary for most Thai to engage in various forms of spirit propitiation. Despite the Buddhist ethic, therefore, it is quite normal for Thai to maintain a little spirit house in a corner of the compound in which one's home is located, and to make offerings in the name of the Buddha to obtain the benevolence of the spirit believed to dominate in the place. Buddhist priests will also perform ceremonies in connection with rice cultivation which, in effect, constitute appeals to pertinent spirits for their cooperation, and the priests also exorcize evil spirits. Similar rituals will be performed to obtain blessings for certain events and to purify locations that presumably have been tainted (for example, by the residence of a leper). In all such practices, the Thai are "buying insurance," in a way. They are also engaging in activities which can be related to the ancient mythology of Hinduism with its pantheon of gods. Such spirit worship, however, like Theravada Buddhism, reinforces in Thai culture the belief that the ethereal forces which control the universe can be aligned with individual welfare by special appeals and nonmaterialistic actions which have little to do with the quality of human labor, rationality, or developed occupational skills.

To the two components of the ethical-religious belief system summarized above must be added the widespread willingness to give some credence to such pseudo-sciences as astrology, numerology, palmistry, and fortune-telling. The beliefs associated with these practices do not so much involve an appeal to supernatural forces to shape events favorably as they do an attempt to divine the most propitious time to engage in certain activities, avoid others, and generally relate one's behavior to "scientific" analysis of the working of the universe. Some degree of belief in these methods for promoting one's well-being cuts across almost all levels of society. It frequently constitutes a basis for decision not only by rice farmers but by senior government officials in both their private lives and their occupations. Once again, sanction for such beliefs is obtained from some Buddhist priests who acquire reputations as diviners of the unknown through one or another of these methods. The conflict of values with those of Western rationalism is clear, but this does not lessen the importance in Thai culture of these techniques. It does mean, however, that the belief in these practices may be concealed from Westerners by educated Thai. In any event, as in all other facets of the ethical-religious belief system, emphasis is placed upon individual, nonmaterial effort to gain personal security and well-being.

GENERAL THAI VALUES

There are certain other values and attitudes which, although rooted to varying degrees in the ethical-religious belief system, have emerged primarily as general products of human interaction within the total Thai and Asian context. Chief among these are the concepts of the "cool heart" and of "face."

The attitude which has been referred to as that of the "cool heart" represents the idealized Thai view of skillful behavior in human relations. It offers to the Thai, in effect, the best means of engaging successfully in individual gamesmanship. The person with a "cool heart" is one who has achieved emotional self-control and the peculiar type of psychic security and capacity to remain uninvolved which is advocated by Theravada Buddhism. Moderate, nonviolent, and able to employ the common Thai expression "never mind" ("mai pen rai") in all embarrassing, difficult, and unstable situations, such a person is able to demonstrate his superiority over all others with whom he is in contact. This, in a way, also constitutes the maximization of the Thai approach to individualism—the ability to protect one's own "face" in human relationships while, simultaneously, compelling competitors to lose some through evidences of lesser self-control. The concept of the "cool heart" also lies behind the maximization of efforts to control facial and verbal reactions to difficult situations; to be "enigmatic," in the view of Westerners. It is an important aspect of the unverbalized communications system in which competing Thai engage and through which they attempt to establish superiority over each other.

The concept of "face" is closely associated with the "cool heart." It, too, is related to individualism and the sense of individual dignity. A Thai does not wish to lose "face"—be obviously embarrassed or otherwise have his dignity or status impaired. This attitude may go so far as his not wanting to engage in a private self-analysis whose result might be inimical to his own self-image; there are, for example, evidences of senior government officials refusing to take examinations in advanced government-training programs even though they would grade their own tests, and no one else would know the results.

Not only are the Thai anxious to protect their personal "face"; they also wish to help protect that of friends as well as of superiors against whom they have no overriding grievances. It is for this reason that they are reluctant to undertake actions or say things which, they feel, might be embarrassing to the other person in a particular relationship. This protective attitude concerning the "face" of superiors undoubtedly is related to the Thai belief in the natural basis of hierarchy—a desire not to cause people whose virtue is demonstrated by their superior status to lose "face." The concepts of the "cool heart" and of "face," therefore, are critical elements in Thai behavior.

An additional behavioral attitude also should be noted in connection with this web of values which governs human relationships. It is the attitude that there is nothing wrong with taking advantage of another person's lack of virtue—his greed, ignorance, or incompetence—in furthering oneself. This is viewed as an important skill of human relations, to be admired rather than condemned, and one which is justified by the Theravada-Buddhist ethic.

The complex of values and attitudes suggested above is important not only in any analysis of the general Thai culture but also, specifically, of the political culture. For it provides important behavioral guides to the relationships among Thai and between Thai and non-Thai in political-administrative dealings. All of these values help to define, from the Thai perspective, the characteristics of an admirable administrative superior or government leader. Such imagery surrounding the performance of the leadership role is part of the Thai definition of "good" leadership. Significantly, this traditional view does not place stress primarily on job efficiency or career advancement through tangible accomplishment.

CULTURAL FLEXIBILITY AND CULTURAL COHESION

Finally, it is important to take note of the selective cultural flexibility which has characterized the Thai people in conjunction with their cultural cohesion. While possessed of a complex network of values, attitudes, and beliefs which has provided them with cultural integrity and the basis for nationhood, the lack of dogmatism and of preoccupation with doctrinal purity also has permitted the Thai to be reasonably moderate and pragmatic in reacting to peoples of other cultures. They have not been driven by a strong desire to force their culture upon others, and they have been willing to excuse violations of their own behavioral guidelines by foreigners in their midst. Moreover, they have demonstrated a measure of receptivity to useful foreign concepts and techniques. Thus, it has been possible in the past for other cultures to penetrate the Thai value system when the behavior manifested could produce specific results of interest to the Thai. Under royal leadership prior to 1932, therefore, governmentally useful foreign practices were assimilated from China, India, the Khmer empire, and Western Europe. Facilitated by their cultural respect for the judgment of hierarchical leadership, the Thai also have demonstrated since 1850 a willingness to respond to economic incentives in the field of agriculture and increasingly to engage in specialized agricultural production geared to high export prices. Moreover, since World War II they have indicated a willingness to employ new cultivation techniques which can increase agricultural productivity, and they have responded favorably to government programs designed to encourage agricultural diversification.

Nevertheless, it must also be noted that the range of Thai cultural diversity and pragmatism demonstrated to date is restricted. The types of modernizing change to which they have accommodated in the past have not been revolutionary—they have not been so drastic that they have seriously conflicted with deeply held beliefs or traditional behavior patterns. As yet, for example, there has been no great eagerness on the part of large numbers of Thai to engage in industry or commerce, as the Japanese have done. What appears to be indicated, therefore, is that while Thai culture is susceptible to a measure of change when such is encouraged by governmental authorities, this cultural capacity for adjustment, adaptation, and assimilation is greatest when associated with traditional behavior and interests. The willingness to accept a major cultural renovation, however, remains uncertain.

Social Factors

The social context for considering contemporary Thailand's development problems and prospects can best be analyzed in two major respects: ethnic majority-minority relationships and social structures.

ETHNIC MAJORITY-MINORITY RELATIONSHIPS

As suggested earlier, Thailand has made considerable progress in establishing that social, psychological, and cultural foundation on which nationhood is based. As a result, it already has gone a long way toward acquiring this vital prerequisite to modernity. In so doing, it also has obtained such important benefits as stability and the existence of a national will to survive in independence. Thailand, therefore, has proved to be culturally and socially, as well as politically and economically, a viable national unit up to the present time.

Nevertheless, in the contemporary era it has become increasingly apparent that major gaps do exist in the effective socialization of important segments of the resident population. Under current international conditions, these gaps threaten national security. Moreover, they prevent large numbers of people from making appropriate contributions to national development and defense through effective participation in the primary structural systems of society. What are these problem areas?

Throughout its long history, nation-building in Thailand has been greatly facilitated by the fact that there is an ethnic, cultural, and religious majority which, at its outer limits, constitutes about 85 percent of the total population. This Greater Thai group, however, is effectively integrated only in the case of that 60 percent of the total population which belongs to three of its four ethnic subgroups: the "central" Thai, "northern" Thai, and "Korat" Thai. Collectively, these three subgroups form the country's strategic cultural core. Among them, the fifteen million central Thai (half the nation's total population)—most of whom inhabit the Chao Phraya Basin and Central Plain, in which Bangkok is located —provide not only cultural but also political, economic, and social leadership. It is these central Thai to which the nation and the country are anchored. They speak the "King's Thai," generally are more worldly as well as more developed (agriculturally, commercially, industrially and culturally), and dominate the country's geopolitical heartland—the great Central Plain with its 71,081 square miles of rich alluvial soil, which revolves about an urban hub, the national capital. It is upon the central Thai, therefore, that Thailand's unity and integrity most depend. Fortunately, they are able to count for support upon the two and one-half million "northern" Thai and two million "Korat" Thai, to whom they are intimately related as members of the same ethnic, linguistic, and cultural family. Collectively, they are the source of that broad consensus which has characterized the society.

Unfortunately, however, it also has become increasingly apparent during the past decade that the fourth ethnic subgroup of the Greater Thai people resident in Thailand (other members outside the country include the Lao in Laos, the Shans of Burma, the Thai who remained in South China, and the Tai tribes along China's southern perimeter from Burma to Vietnam) has not been as well integrated. This subgroup is comprised of the roughly eight million "Thai-Lao," who form more than 25 percent of the total population and 40 percent of the Greater Thai family.

The Thai-Lao, although ethnically and culturally related to

all Thai, have a distinctive language and script which is not completely intelligible to the other Thai. Even more important, however, is the fact that they are concentrated in the economically most depressed area of the country (the Northeast). Living primarily on the Korat Plateau and adjoining land along the Mekong River Boundary with Laos, their arid homeland has been incapable of providing a standard of living (including health and education) comparable to that of the rest of the population. The government, for example, has recently noted that annual per capita income has been about $45 in the Northeast, compared to well over $100 for the rest of the country. However, until recently, that same government has paid little attention to the region's economic problems. Also it has not, in the past, been particularly interested in socializing the Thai-Lao more completely into the national culture. Instead, the Thai-Lao, while not actively discriminated against, have been treated as culturally inferior "country cousins," for whom it was not necessary to provide social services comparable to— let alone greater than—those given the other Thai.

The fact that the Thai-Lao's depressed condition was producing smoldering resentments became politically evident a decade ago when elections for the National Assembly still were permitted (the last regular Constitution was abrogated in 1959). At that time, and despite heavy-handed government control and manipulation, the chosen representatives from the Northeast became the primary spokesmen for economic and social radicalism, often referring to themselves as socialists.

Today, the Thai-Lao have become a source of concern for national security reasons. Their long-standing grievances are being stimulated and possibly exploited by Communists who infiltrate from neighboring Laos and talk of the need to create a new and "greater" Laos within which all Lao people would be joined in freedom from Bangkok and imperialist "oppression." Confronted by this separatist threat at a time when Red China also is openly calling for the destruction of the Thai regime, the government in

Bangkok must engage in major programs of cultural, economic, social, psychological, and political integration and development if the Thai-Lao are to become active members of the Thai community rather than rebels in a Communist revolutionary war. Efforts are being made (these are discussed in Chapter VI), but their adequacy and effectiveness remain uncertain after a lengthy history of disinterest.

The Chinese in Thailand present a second serious minority problem of a somewhat different nature. Both numerically and economically, they are the most important of the non-Thai ethnic groups resident in the country. Although some Chinese were present even in ancient times, they entered Thailand in large numbers primarily under the government's program of modernization and development during the mid-nineteenth century. This mass movement was looked upon with favor by the Thai kings, for the Chinese were willing to perfom the new economic roles of wage labor and commercial trading which the agrarian Thai were not.

In the first part of the twentieth century, however, the Chinese became less welcome in Thailand. A new Thai nationalism was being cultivated by the monarchy as part of the modernization process. The Chinese began bringing wives from their motherland and intermarrying less frequently with the Thai. As a result, by World War I, the process of Chinese assimilation had slowed considerably. The tensions between these two increasingly autonomous communities hardened and, beginning in 1926, the Thai government launched a series of efforts both to reduce the flow of Chinese and to control those already within the country. By 1947, therefore, Chinese immigration was officially limited to 10,000 annually, while subsequent legislation also sought to restrict the number of occupations in which they could engage. Nevertheless, there are now an estimated three million ethnic Chinese resident in Thailand, approximately 410,000 of whom (according to the 1960 census) actually hold alien citizenship. Whether citizen or alien, however, the Chinese of Thailand still constitute a distinct ethnic and cultural minority who represent a potential threat to Thai national security as well as a serious problem for Thai economic development.

One element of the Chinese problem derives from the fact that their economic vigor and commercial ability, combined with traditional Thai distaste for nonagricultural pursuits, have enabled them to gain a position of great economic and financial power within the society. Thus, despite all restrictive legislation, the ethnic Chinese currently compose some 60 to 70 percent of all nonagricultural labor and 90 percent of all skilled labor. They are, therefore, the dominant component of what little there is in the way of a modern Thai labor force. In addition, ethnic Chinese entrepreneurs own so large a percentage of the rice mills (80%), saw mills, rubber plantations, tin mines, processing plants and factories, banking and credit facilities, and they form so great a percentage of the small retail business and artisan groups, that they are the major component of the small nonbureaucratic urban middle and upper-middle class.

This Chinese economic dominance is a problem because much of the Chinese community is not effectively socialized and assimilated into Thai society. Although improvement in the process of assimilation has been occurring, and the younger generation of Chinese are seeking a place as Thai citizens, the process obviously must be expanded considerably.

The second major reason for the Chinese problem, a reason directly related to the first, stems from the emergence of an aggressive, expansionist Communist China. Obviously, with significant elements of this economically powerful minority only partially assimilated into Thai society and historically characterized by their ties with and pride in the culture of their traditional homeland, there are serious possibilities of subversion against the Thai state. Communist infiltration of some urban Chinese workers undoubtedly has occurred, and there has been evidence of a degree of infiltration of intellectual and commercial groups as well. While no one can demonstrate conclusively that a majority of the Chinese in Thailand have been affected, the importance of the Chinese role clearly presents the Thai state with a major problem whose resolution must be the further effective assimilation of the Chinese. A new Thai approach based upon something more positive than restrictive legislation is necessary both for national security and for national development.

The third minor ethnic group which presents Thailand with some potentially significant security and development problems is composed of the estimated 800,000 Thai-Malays. These people, who are followers of Islam, comprise about 80 percent of the population in the four southern provinces of Thailand bordering on Malaysia. Their first language is Malay, and they are essentially unintegrated into Thai society. Although their simple mining and agrarian economic activities are compatible with Thai activities, and Thailand and Malaysia presently maintain good relations, there is a potential for irredentism as long as they remain generally outside the Thai community. Occasionally, moreover, there are increasing evidences of Communist and separatist forces at work among these people. What is required, therefore, is a positive Thai program which integrates them more effectively into the society without infringing upon their existing religious freedom or cultural distinctiveness.

SOCIAL STRUCTURES

The traditional social structures which developed prior to 1850 were well rooted in the culture, religious beliefs, and agricultural economy of old Siam. They also were a product of the several governmental systems created both in South China and during the Thai people's first 600 years in Southeast Asia.

In the Sukhothai kingdom (ca. 1238–1350), there was a feudal-type system of territorial administration and socio-economic organization under which the various provinces were governed by semihereditary nobles loyal to the king, who was a paternalistic "father of the people." The major nobility, in turn, received the allegiance of lesser warrior nobles who operated agricultural estates to which the peasantry was attached.

During the subsequent Ayudhyan era (1350–1767), however, the monarch became a demigod entitled to total obedience from a state and society which were highly centralized and bureaucratized. Assimilating various governmental and administrative techniques from the conquered Khmer empire, royal power was manifested in social, political, and religious spheres of life. To increase societal integration and administrative efficiency in this much larger state, the semifeudal nobility were transformed into government officials, while the peasants were freed from the land and bound directly to the king for purposes of allegiance, taxes, and various required services. In addition, in Ayudhya, every adult male was ranked and incorporated on a national level, into a social, economic, and governmental hierarchy. Under this system (which ended only in 1932), a person's rank consisted of his title, his official position in the bureaucracy, the royal name given him by the king, and his number of "dignity marks." These "dignity marks" were originally determined by the number of *rai* of land granted an individual by the king. The ordinary person had 25 *rai* (about 10 acres of land) while the head of a government department would have 10,000 and a powerful prince, 100,000. Subsequently, these *sakdi na* numbers were assigned on the basis of one's position in society and without reference to land. Officials with more than 400 were appointed directly by the king as a sort of "commissioned officer" group. To avoid a rigidly stratified social system, however, members of the royal family and nobility also were subject to a system of downgrading which made them commoners after five generations. Moreover, official titles and positions were not inherited: Persons assumed as names the titles attached to their current positions and changed them when they obtained new government posts. All inherited wealth also was divided equally among the sons of a family.

When the Chakri dynasty (1767 to the present) began the process of modernization in the mid-nineteenth century, a large proportion of the population were slaves of one form or another while almost all adult males sixteen years of age or older were subject to the *corvée*—the required several months of personal service to the king. Slavery had become common prior to 1874, according to authoritative analysis, primarily for the economic security and protection which it provided. Free men thus sold themselves into slavery, and an elaborate body of law existed which governed the rights and conditions of the various kinds of slaves. Rama V (King Chulalongkorn) began the termination of slavery by a decree of 1874 which freed people born into slavery after October 1, 1868 on their twenty-first birthday, and prohibited the sale of persons who reached twenty-one years of age after that same date. A later decree covered additional groups and finally, in 1905, slavery was completely abolished by law.

The *corvée* system of forced labor also was eliminated by stages throughout the nineteenth century. During the first part of the century, men were permitted to pay money instead of providing the several months of free labor. Under Rama IV (King Mongkut), the state began to pay a fixed wage to conscripted labor, and paid free labor was employed when available. In 1899, a law established a head tax to replace the *corvée* system, with persons defaulting in such payments being required to provide thirty days' service. This penalty was reduced to fifteen days in 1926 and, in 1938, the capitation tax itself was also eliminated. Thus, by this abolition both of slavery and of the *corvée* system, Thai labor was freed in a major modification of the traditional social and economic systems.

Contemporary Thai social structures generally reflect both the cultural, economic, and political modifications of traditional society which have occurred since 1850 and those traditional characteristics which have been retained. The social system, therefore, has remained well integrated with the other major structural-functional systems. However, while this integration has contributed to the country's stability, it also represents another key area in which some change is essential for further development.

As one surveys the contemporary social system, several features are particularly significant: (1) the overwhelming majority of the population, as members of rural society, are involved in social structures which, like their economic and political structures, are still very close to the traditional; (2) the major distinction within contemporary Thai society is between the rural and urban sectors, with the latter being more elaborately structured and also more reflective of the modernizing forces within the country; (3) there are, as yet, no significant socio-economic groups which are sufficiently frustrated and alienated from the society to spearhead real social, economic, or political revolution; (4) the major inadequacy of the contemporary social system is the absence of a significant nonbureaucratic Thai middle class capable of spearheading the modernization and development movement.

Thus, the social system within which 85 percent of the population lives even today is shaped to a major extent by their traditional form of agricultural existence, as previously suggested. It is also, of course, completely intertwined with the traditional religious beliefs and cultural characteristics portrayed earlier. An outstanding feature of this rural society is its relative classlessness in Western terms. For, with almost 90 percent of all Thai farmers owning their land, and with few tenant farmers or farm laborers, rural Thailand is composed chiefly of small, independent farmers whose economic condition is one neither of extreme wealth nor of extreme poverty. This relative economic equality at a level of well-being which is high for Asia has contributed much to the complacency and calm marking human relationships. Conditions in the Thai countryside have not in the past provided the basis for agrarian revolt, even in the Northeast.

The relative economic equality of rural Thailand also has meshed well with Theravada Buddhism's assertion of mankind's moral equality and its equation of moral virtue and social status. From this web of economic practice and religious belief has emerged not only a relatively classless and quiescent rural society but one characterized by its emphasis on individual self-reliance and belief in a moral basis for economic and social equality of opportunity. The Thai behave, therefore, as relatively autonomous individuals rather than as members of classes or of broad socioeconomic interest groups. Their acceptance of authority and hierarchy, moreover, still is generally rooted in the belief that high social status and wealth are manifestations of ethical virtue which has been individually earned.

The important social differences which do exist in rural Thailand, then, are not so much a result of economics as they are of the traditional culture and the Ayudhyan heritage. With the 1932 abandonment of the old *sakdi na* system of ranking the citizenry, an individual's social status has since been determined by a combination of the following criteria: (1) age—advanced age automatically being accorded respect since it connotes wisdom borne of experience with life; (2) sex—although women have a strong social and economic position, they traditionally manifest respect for men who, alone, can enter the Buddhist clergy; (3) membership in the Buddhist clergy—both monks and novices are accorded great respect and have high prestige; (4) occupation—farming, and particularly rice cultivation, as well as government employment, carry high prestige while commercial and industrial activities do not.

The status and power elites of rural Thailand are, therefore, the government officials, who administer the provinces, districts, and communes; the locally selected village headmen, who are customarily chosen by and drawn from the ranks of the village elders; the village elders themselves, who normally are the most successful local farmers; and the Buddhist clergy. The actual economic gap between these elites and the rest of rural society is relatively small. Moreover, additional social flexibility is provided by the fact that other individuals who are not members of the local elites can nevertheless acquire high social status through evidence of Buddhist merit or because of personal skills which are valued in the community. Thus, for the overwhelming majority of Thai, the farmers, the prevailing social stratification within their communities has ethical and traditional rather than socio-economic or class implications.

The greatest breach within the contemporary Thai social system is that between the rural society and the limited number of urban areas—this because the latter manifest most of the transitional features of the country which have emerged since 1850. Urban Thai society, and particularly that of Bangkok, is much more stratified and its values and attitudes are more permeated by Chinese and Western cultures than is the case in the simpler and more isolated countryside. Bangkok society, therefore, does reveal a more elaborate hierarchy of social status groups. Nevertheless, although these groups do reflect a greater spread in wealth, power, prestige, and behavior patterns than is true of rural Thailand, they also are not true classes in the traditional European sense.

Analytically, five broad status groups can be discerned in Bangkok, and all tend to have somewhat higher prestige than comparable groups elsewhere in the country because of the city's position as the center of governmental, social, cultural, and religious leadership. The relationships among these status groups are flexible, however, and sufficient individual mobility exists often to blur the distinctions. Moreover, the determinants of status still include traditional Thai factors, and the system remains anchored to the national culture and heritage. Nevertheless, the blend of traditional and Western value systems has produced an intermingling of such criteria for status as wealth, talent, family connections, religious behavior, education, political power, and governmental position.

The distinguishable urban groups, in descending order of social status, are the aristocracy (the royal family and traditional nobility); the new commoner elite (top military, political, administrative, professional, and business leaders); the upper middle class (intermediate-level civil servants, military officers, professionals, teachers, merchants, small businessmen, and white collar workers); a lower middle class (overwhelmingly Chinese and composed chiefly of craftsmen and skilled laborers); and a lower class (unskilled laborers, domestic help, peddlers, etc.). The king is at the pinnacle of the social structure and the Buddhist clergy has extremely high social status, although outside the secular structure.

Both Thai and Chinese citizens are found at all urban status levels except among the aristocracy (who are exclusively Thai) and the senior military and civil bureaucracy (also Thai). Access to the highest levels of urban society is obtained by Thai primarily through bureaucratic position (military and civil) or through political power. For the Chinese, however, access is gained mainly through economic position and its related influence on the occupiers of top official posts.

Despite the emergence of a more modern set of urban elites whose values and behavior no longer are exclusively traditional in character, the social and economic basis for vigorous reformation and modernization of Thai society does not yet exist. To a great extent, this results from the fact that both the masses and the elites of present-day Thailand are still reasonably well satisfied with things as they are. Those energetic and achievement-oriented individuals who do emerge either in rural or in urban Thailand generally have not faced the types of overwhelming frustration which would alienate them from the present system and direct them toward major modernization efforts. Moreover, given Thai individualism, there has been little tendency for such individuals to coalesce into anything approaching a stable and coherent group.

The most distinguishing features of the ruling segment of society have been its advanced education and its bureaucratic or official nature. However, through steady expansion of the formal educational system, achievement-oriented individuals have gained access to advanced educational opportunities and hence have been able to mount this primary social escalator. Moreover, with social stratification relatively blurred even in Bangkok, and entry into the bureaucracy open to those with formal education, such individuals have been able to obtain satisfaction of their ambitions within the system and without resort to major attacks upon it.

75

The one great exception to this social mobility of modern Thailand—the career frustration of the commoner civil and military elites in the 1920's—did indeed produce, in 1932, a successful coup d'etat against the aristocratic oligarchy which had gained control of the Thai state. Nevertheless, this attack upon the existing order was not an historic revolution. Ultimately, it represented not a complete overturning of the traditional order so much as a seizure of supreme political power by second-echelon bureaucrats whose collective commitment to modernization proved to be limited chiefly to satisfaction of their own bureaucratic ambitions. Since 1932, they and their successors have tended to continue at a slower pace the earlier royal approach to modernization: namely, governmental, legal, and administrative reform designed to facilitate Thai adaptation to new internal and external pressures without actually promoting changes which might cause any drastic transformation of society or otherwise undermine the country's traditional stability.

Socio-economic pressures for extensive modernization also have not yet been generated because no significant, stable, urban industrial labor force or nonbureaucratic middle class has developed. Urban workers represent only about 3 percent of the total Thai work force, they are not effectively organized either into a labor party or into trade unions, and most skilled urban workers are Chinese and so are suspect by most Thai. Hence, they exert little economic or political influence in behalf of change. Nor is there as yet any real Thai middle class in the Western sense. As already noted, the Chinese constitute the key private entrepreneurial element in Thailand, to date, and their ability to provide leadership in any major modernization effort is limited both by their own cultural preoccupation with family enterprise and their tangential role in Thai society. The only equivalent of a Thai middle class is provided by the second-echelon civil and military officials of the state, and they are reasonably well satisfied as long as their individual official careers prosper. The very success of Thai society and the polity in socializing most achievement-oriented individuals and in providing them with bureaucratic outlets for their aspirations thus has reduced the ability of the country to engage in vigorous self-modernization.

Clearly, therefore, Thailand needs a greatly expanded and non-bureaucratic entrepreneurial class which would be willing to play the catalytic role necessary to further development. However, since the emergence of such a class depends upon major modifications of Thai culture as well as additional economic growth, for the foreseeable future the strategic leadership must somehow be developed within the existing bureaucratic elites.

Economic Factors

Contemporary Thailand certainly is experiencing the gradual growth of new domestic pressures for economic development, even though these pressures are not yet overwhelming. They derive primarily from (1) the steady diminution of that favorable ratio of natural resources to population which has been a key element in the country's economic well-being and development up to this point; (2) the emergence of what may prove to be adverse long-term international market conditions for the major Thai exports of the past 160 or more years; (3) the growth in popular consumer appetites, which have been whetted and diversified as the society and economy have become more involved in international trade and communications; (4) the mounting needs of the Thai government for greater income in order to meet the financial requirements for improved national defense, social welfare, modern public administration, and economic development; (5) the emerging security danger to the Thai state which derives, in part, from the specific economic underdevelopment of important resident-ethnic minorities such as the Thai-Lao of the Northeast and the Thai-Malay of the South; (6) the growing discontent of small urban intellectual groups who desire the general modernization and economic development of the kingdom.

The fact that these pressures for economic development have

not yet become overwhelming, and that there is still sufficient time for Thailand to make the necessary economic development effort, is attributable largely to the natural economic strength of the country up to the present. Prior to 1850, the kingdom was virtually self-sufficient and had consciously avoided for at least a century having any extensive contact with the more economically dynamic and aggressive West. With an estimated five to six million people, it was sparsely populated, almost all of the economically active population was engaged in agriculture and particularly in rice cultivation, and rice production reportedly was sufficient not only to feed the country but to export large quantities to meet South Chinese needs, as well. The Thai peasantry, moreover, also met its own requirements for such other products as cotton, silk, tobacco, sugar cane, fruit, spices, and vegetables. A local cottage and village textile industry clothed them, simple locally produced farm implements were employed, the water buffalo provided supplemental power, extensive fishing resources were available in inland waterways as well as on the seacoasts, local timber was available for construction, and supplemental household items were obtained through barter primarily within the villages themselves. With a tropical climate, extensive waterways, heavy monsoon rains, large areas of fertile soil, and human needs defined primarily in subsistence terms, traditional Siam was economically stable and relatively content.

What foreign trade there was prior to 1850 existed primarily with Asian neighbors—the Thai exporting such items as rice, sugar, tobacco, pepper, raw cotton, fish, animal hides and skins, and woods while importing lesser amounts (in value) of such consumer items as textiles, chinaware and crockery, and hardware. Royal revenues were derived from this favorable balance of foreign trade, taxes on agricultural produce, export and import duties, inland-transit duties on goods moving over land and water routes, profits from government trading, and payments in kind or in money from the populace in lieu of providing the required *corvée* to the king. Government expenditures were devoted largely to the maintenance of the royal court and officials, the financing of wars, the construction and maintenance of Buddhist religious buildings, and limited public works such as the construction of canals for irrigation and transportation. The *corvée* system provided unpaid labor for construction activities.

The Bowring Treaty with Great Britain in 1856 opened Thailand to extensive trade with the West, establishing a pattern which subsequently was followed in a series of similar treaties with some fourteen other countries, including Japan. The results, as analyzed and documented by James C. Ingram,[3] were to move Thailand into that transitional stage of economic development in which it still functions. Foreign trade increased significantly, and the Thai population became less self-sufficient because of specialization for export in rice cultivation and the production of a few primary products like teak, tin, and, after World War I, rubber. Partially entering into a market and money economy, the mounting sums of foreign exchange were used to finance an increasing variety of consumer imports. The new exchange sectors of the economy, in turn, generated new economic functions which were filled by middlemen (mainly Chinese immigrants). Simultaneously, the royal government, under the leadership first of Rama IV (King Mongkut) and then of Rama V (King Chulalongkorn) and Rama VI (King Wachirawut), actively promoted various forms of administrative, legal and judicial, fiscal and economic modernization—some of which were necessitated by the treaties imposed by Western powers and some of which derived from royal conviction that Thailand had to modernize in order to avoid the fate of China and the neighboring Southeast Asian states.

Nevertheless, despite such limited economic development since 1850, largely in response to external pressures and stimuli, the Thai economy has remained firmly linked to most of its traditional characteristics. There has not been any dramatic progress in the form of major increases in per capita income and, at least until the

[3] See James C. Ingram, *Economic Change in Thailand Since 1850* (Stanford, Calif.: Stanford University Press, 1955), pp. 6–35, for an authoritative discussion of the traditional economy and its transformation between 1850 and 1950.

advent of the 1960's, according to Ingram, "not much 'development' in the sense of the utilization of more capital, relative to labor, and of new techniques." [4] The economic growth until relatively recently has been chiefly "natural"—a result of willingness by Thai farmers to produce rice and a few other primary products for the world market as well as a reflection of the extent to which the increasing population, to date, could be absorbed into an agrarian economy by the expedient of opening up additional land for cultivation. As yet, there has been no real technological revolution, even in agriculture, and only minimal industrialization.

Now, however, the favorable combination of natural circumstances which has provided the historic underpinning for Thai economic well-being, as well as for the country's social and political stability, is diminishing. As analyzed by a professional team of the International Bank for Reconstruction and Development several years ago, the key favorable elements of the economy are losing their force.[5] Most of the good rice land is occupied, average rice yields have remained relatively static for a number of years, most of the accessible teak forests have been cut and decades are needed to regenerate them, adverse long-term world market conditions prevail in the tin industry, and the population is growing by at least 2.5 to 3 percent annually. Given the continuation of these tendencies without major modification and modernization of the economy, Thailand will have to devote an increasing proportion of its rice production to feed its own people. This will make necessary a reduction in exports, and may even, ultimately, confront the country with serious domestic rice shortages. No longer relatively isolated and insulated from the world economy and its currents, no longer as self-sufficient as it used to be, Thailand actually faces the possibility of long-term economic deterioration unless a significant development program is conducted by the

[4] *Ibid.*, p. 216.
[5] International Bank for Reconstruction and Development, *A Public Development Program for Thailand* (Baltimore: Johns Hopkins University Press, 1959), Chapter 1, pp. 1–32.

government. That program must provide additional social overhead capital facilities, new investment capital, and legal and structural reforms. Fortunately, action is being taken (see Chapter VI). Its adequacy in terms of the challenges facing the country remains open to question, however.

CHAPTER IV

❦

The Contemporary
Political System

Government is the critical variable in the development of societies, particularly in the contemporary era. As the authoritative leadership core of the polity (political system) and thereby of the entire society, it alone is in a position to mobilize, stimulate, and channel all of a country's human and natural resources for development purposes. In an age in which non-Western peoples increasingly desire in a matter of decades what the West has created over a 300-year period, and when some of these benefits must actually materialize rapidly if some countries are to survive, many societies must turn to government for leadership.

This leadership role of government does not mean that developing countries must have some specific form of totalitarian, dictatorial, or even of democratic socialist or liberal democratic regime. Many of the new states, in fact, already have demonstrated that, apart from existing cultural obstacles, they are not modern enough or developed enough to operate European-style socialism, Anglo-American democracy, or totalitarianism successfully. What are really required are creative mixes of public and private activity under dynamic, effective, and popular government. To that end, government can and should serve in these under-developed lands as resource mobilizer, stimulator, educator, facili-tator, and regulator, selectively supplementing and encouraging (not automatically preventing) the growth of useful private enter-prise. For most contemporary countries—given their degree of underdevelopment, the problems they face, their current lack of alternative sources of leadership, and time pressures—there is little other choice but for government to take the leadership role in development.

What about Thailand, then? What is the nature of the Thai polity and its government, and to what extent has it been suffi-ciently modernized to play the role of developer? Put another way, does the Thai government have the required capabilities to provide the necessary leadership for national development and, thereby, for national security? How does one evaluate its strengths and its weaknesses? Much of our estimate of the extent to which Thailand may become another Vietnam depends on this evalua-tion.

General Characteristics

Because Thailand's contemporary political system—a limited monarchy governed as a moderate military dictatorship—is well rooted in the country's culture and traditions, it has benefited, like the predecessor regimes, from a large measure of popular con-sensus or at least acquiescence. Nevertheless, this regime, too, con-tains the seeds of its own destruction—in part of its own making —just as did the absolute monarchy before it.

For one thing, the 1932 coup which created the regime was conducted under the European-style banners of modernization and parliamentary democracy. Although there was no popular par-ticipation in the coup and little mass enthusiasm for these causes has been developed since then, neither of these major justifications for establishing the new regime really has been honored very much. At some point in time, therefore, the current system could be called to account for its failures in achieving proclaimed goals. In addition, members of the ruling circle of the new elite have only a limited historic basis for legitimizing their present leadership roles. They can draw upon traditional respect for authority, acceptance of hierarchy, and the royal conferral of their ministerial offices, but it is also clear that their leadership positions up to now are actually based chiefly upon seizure of power in coups. Finally, each new ruling group tends to justify its assumption of power and seeks to enhance its claims by public exposure of the corruption, incompetence, and undemocratic character of its predecessors. This tactic is bound, in the long run, to raise serious questions among the general citizenry as to the actual legitimacy and moral virtue of all leadership since 1932. Such questions certainly have already crossed the minds of some of the country's best educated, urbanized, and westernized elements.

To overcome these weaknesses, the contemporary Thai political system seeks to unite the traditional with the modern by employing some Western organizational forms and by functioning through improvised interpersonal and intergroup arrangements which conform to existing power realities. Unfortunately, however, this type of intermingling of the traditional and the modern has not yet produced a stable new political alloy. The traditional, transitional, and modern are interacting, but they have not been effectively blended and institutionalized to meet the nation's contemporary and, particularly, its future political requirements. As in the past, the government still remains supreme, the social and economic structures subordinate, and the society reasonably complacent. But Thailand has not yet developed a truly stable and effective replacement for the absolute monarchy. It is, after all, a self-proclaimed constitutional monarchy which, for the past ten years, has been functioning without a real constitution. Instead, it has been governed since 1958 under a seventh and "interim" constitutional statement which abrogated the previous Constitution, authorized the government to appoint (not elect) all members of the National (Constituent) Assembly, and empowered the Prime Minister—the commander-in-chief of the Armed Forces who had seized power in a coup—to rule by decree whenever he felt it to be necessary in order to preserve law and order or the national security. The same government also has banned political parties, trade unions, and elections during this period. It has finally (at the end of 1967) produced a new draft for a "permanent" constitution which presumably will be put into force during 1968, but it is also quite clear that the militarized oligarchy which has run the country most of the time since 1932 has little intention of transferring actual power. The terms, "democracy" and "socialism," have been employed frequently during the past twenty-five years, but the transfer of political power by coup d'etat has been normal. Although Westerners regularly refer to the regime as one of the most stable in the underdeveloped world, it has not as yet resolved such basic political problems as the regularization of succession to national leadership, the appropriate internal structuring of the political system for policy formulation and decision-making, and the proper relationship between the political leadership and the citizenry. The system's incongruities, therefore, are very great and are open to exploitation by political critics, opponents, and revolutionaries, whether completely indigenous or externally sponsored.

The overriding political reality of contemporary Thailand, then, is that for three decades it has been governed through improvised political structures which clearly lack most of the ideological substance of the 1932 "revolution." The fact that this has been possible, and has been accomplished with so little difficulty, is certainly evidence of the great cultural, social, and economic stability which has always characterized Thai society. Moreover, it also indicates something of the critical role played by the governmental bureaucracy, whose considerable experience and elitist position enables it to keep the state functioning in basic terms. Nevertheless, the ability of the Thai polity to provide the necessary leadership through such improvisations becomes increasingly questionable as both internal and external pressures for change intensify. The country's continued survival in independence thus requires more permanent, more developed, and more efficient political-governmental structures. Otherwise, the historic success of Thai society may be shattered by new revolutionary forces which gradually are making their appearance within the country, stimulated by movements which are sweeping through Southeast Asia and the entire underdeveloped world, and focused by Communist activities. What are the current capabilities of the Thai polity to promote that additional degree of national development on which the country's future survival in independence and prosperity is heavily dependent? How effective is it as a leadership and problem-solving system?

Integrative Capabilities

TERRITORIAL INTEGRATION

The contemporary Thai solution to the problem of territorial integration is unitary in nature. As such, it is a continuation of the centralization introduced during the Ayudhyan era and modernized by the absolute Chakri kings during the eighteenth and nineteenth centuries. Under the system developed since 1932,[1] general territorial administration is organized in terms of 71 provinces (*changwads*), which are subdivided into 489 districts (*amphurs*), with 8 to 13 districts per province. There are also 34 subdistricts; 4,891 communes (*tambols*), which are groupings of villages averaging 20 per district; and 41,389 villages and hamlets (*mubans*), composed of at least five households each. In addition, there are three categories of municipalities (*tesaban*), which total 120, plus 401 lesser incorporated urban areas, called sanitary districts (*sukaphiban*). The various national ministries operate field

---

[1] For a discussion of territorial administration, see Daniel Wit, *Local Government in Thailand* (Bangkok: Department of Interior, 1958); Malai Huvanandana and William J. Siffin, *Public Administration in Thailand* (Bangkok: Institute of Public Administration, Thammasat University, 1960); and essays by Frederick J. Horrigan, "Provincial Government and Administration," pp. 41–72, and John W. Ryan, "Municipal Government and Administration," pp. 73–121, in J. L. Sutton, ed., *Problems of Politics and Administration in Thailand* (Bloomington: Institute of Training for Public Service, Indiana University, 1962).

units within these territorial entities, and such field units actually employ some 70 percent of the national civil service.

The provinces are headed by provincial governors who are appointed by the Minister of Interior and are responsible to him. The governors supervise the administration of national laws and regulations within their provinces, seek to coordinate the field operations of the national ministries, and exercise certain administrative controls over the municipalities and sanitary districts within their jurisdiction. They are assisted by a council composed of senior representatives of the national ministries functioning within their particular provinces and by provincial police who are tied to the national Police Department of the Ministry of Interior. They are, therefore, both general territorial administrators functioning in behalf of the national government and the coordinators of specialized field activities engaged in by the various ministries. Given the relatively autonomous position of the national ministries and their departments, plus the limited control of funds exercised by the governors, it is not surprising that they face serious difficulties in their coordinating role.

Directly under the governor of each province are district officers, who also are officials of the Ministry of Interior. They perform, within their more limited territorial jurisdiction, the same types of functions as do the governors. Each such officer administers his district; acts as a central government agent for the performance of certain specific functions; attempts to coordinate national departmental field activities; and directly supervises the subdistricts, communes, villages, and hamlets within his jurisdiction.

Each commune has a chief headman (*kamnan*), chosen by village headmen from among their number. Although not a civil servant, the chief headman is paid a small monthly salary as a part-time government employee and serves as the agent of the district officer for information and tax collection purposes. To be appointed, he must be approved by the district officer. The villages, for their part, choose their respective headmen, subject to district officer approval. These headmen also receive a small stipend from the central government. They perform limited administrative functions in behalf of the district officers and are responsible for local law and order.

The Thai municipalities are farthest along the road to local self-government. They are under the immediate supervision of their respective lord mayors (actually appointed by the provincial governors) and councils. Municipal administration is supervised by city clerks and executed by a separate municipal civil service. Nevertheless, all three categories of municipality (depending upon size of population) are subject to tutelary controls exercised by provincial governors and the Department of Interior of the Ministry of Interior. Their functions, adjusted to the size of the municipality, are regulated nationally and their finances are dependent primarily upon central government allocations. Lesser urban areas such as the sanitary districts are administered by boards whose chairmen are the responsible district officers. They, too, are under central tutelage and control similar to that which regulates municipalities.

The outstanding characteristics of territorial and local administration, therefore, obtain from the centralization which prevails. Even with limited decentralization efforts in 1955–1957, and the designation of provinces as legal entities, the governors and district officers, first and foremost, were and are national officers: members of the national civil service operating within the Ministry of Interior. Their functions as local executive officers are secondary to this national role and are not subject to effective local control. Even within the municipalities, national control is preeminent, and the municipality's performance of legally assigned functions is dominated by those national ministries which are, in practice, most concerned with these functions. The regular courts, likewise, are all parts of a national judicial system.

The result of this system, to date, has been a significant degree of territorial integration, legally. Operationally, national control also has been considerable throughout most of the country, the major exception being the hill people in border areas. It must be kept in mind, however, that the national government's interest in the activities of the country's towns and villages (within which most of the populace resides) has been limited chiefly to the maintenance of its legal, fiscal, and general administrative controls plus the provision of a few primary social services (particularly education). Moreover, until the current guerrilla threats began, the national interest has been evidenced least in the Thai-Lao Northeast and the Thai-Malay South. Territorial integration has been maintained, therefore, but it has been fairly relaxed rather than oppressive, totalitarian, or creative. Its effectiveness under the challenge of separatism or of demands for greater local autonomy remains untested, even with new grants of authority to village and provincial leaders in the Northeast.

POLITICIZATION

The ability of the Thai state to politicize its society effectively (to make citizens of its people), like its ability to maintain the country's territorial integrity, has been more dependent upon the general cultural cohesiveness and traditions of the ethnic majority than upon any particularly creative or innovative acts of government. There have been no mass political parties to reach down into the nation's grass roots and no effective incorporation into the national civil service system of the major ethnic minorities; in fact, until the current programs in the Northeast, the only conscious efforts to undercut ethnic alienation have been conducted chiefly in terms of restrictions upon foreign language education (aimed primarily at the private Chinese-language schools). Where nationalistic appeals have been made by government, they have been directed mainly to the Thai majority and often in association with anti-Chinese sentiments. Apart from some pallid and relatively unsuccessful efforts by Field Marshal Phibulsonggram (also known as P[h]ibun[l] and Phibun SongKhram), then Prime Minister, to introduce a degree of neo-fascist symbolism and chauvinism into the Thai system during 1938–1944, and general politicization efforts within the formal educational structures, probably the only conscious attempts to promote national psycho-political integration have been associated with the throne. For, despite the limitations imposed upon the king's powers since 1932, he continues to perform the historic function of symbolizing national unity. He remains the embodiment of the Thai nation: a father-figure and the object of respect from most Thai at all social levels. As a living link to the national history, the monarch is an integral part of Thai political culture. No coup group, therefore, has felt it safe to eliminate the monarchy (it was claimed at various times that both Pridi and Phibun probably would have liked to but dared not). Some regimes, such as that prevailing since 1958, actually have given the royal family increased publicity and freedom of movement in order to take advantage of their symbolic value.

The integrative capabilities developed by the Thai polity, therefore, are minimal. To a great extent, reliance has been placed upon the traditional culture of the majority, with its respect for authority and strong sense of national identity, as well as upon traditional political apathy and socio-economic complacency rooted in reasonably good economic conditions. Government, for its part, generally has taken care to exercise its authority without being oppressive and without seriously disturbing the traditional bases for stability. Even the tax system has not been subjected to thoroughgoing modernization in the past largely because government's reliance primarily upon various indirect taxation techniques has served to conceal its actual impact from the Thai masses. Whether national stability and integration can continue to be maintained by these traditional methods seems doubtful. Newer and more dynamic techniques must be innovated in response to growing challenges to Thai unity.

Educational Capabilities

POLITICAL EDUCATION

The educational capabilities of the Thai polity, as suggested earlier, are most developed in their formal institutional and legal aspects and least in the transmission of popular political education (see pp. 48–50, 52). Both mass literacy and elitist preparation for the civil and military bureaucracy are provided, but there has been little preparation for modern citizenship or for civilian political leadership. This lack of provision for modern political education stems from the fact that while government is authoritarian, it is not modern even in its authoritarianism. There is neither education for a political democracy nor a hierarchy of fascist or communist-type schools for the training of a dictatorial political elite, neither a popular competitive political party system nor a single mass party. There also is no legal trade union movement to provide either political indoctrination in behalf of the regime or to engage in political action in its own behalf. Instead, politics is bureaucratized, militarized, and divorced from the general citizenry. The limited political socialization engaged in by the schools is very general and has been concerned more with Thai culture, history, and traditions than with contemporary political education.

FORMAL EDUCATION

Formal educational capabilities, however, as described earlier (see pp. 47–52), are reasonably good and steadily improving, although they are weak in the preparation of large numbers of Thai for a modern life.[2] The compulsory primary education established by law in 1921 under the absolute monarchy has been enforced with increasing effectiveness since 1935. This is reflected in the fact that by 1961 an estimated 75 percent of children of primary school age were actually in attendance—a very high figure for the non-Western world. Nevertheless, the still prevalent elitist character of society also is revealed by 1961 estimates that only about 120,000 of the estimated 400,000 students who were graduating annually from primary school continued on to secondary school and that, of the 70,000 students who were graduating an-

---

[2] For a summary of the educational system, see Daniel Wit, *Labor Law and Practice in Thailand* (Washington, D.C.: U.S. Department of Labor, Bureau of Labor Statistics Report No. 267, March 1964), Part I, pp. 18–21.

ually from secondary school, probably no more than 10,000 to 15,000 actually entered a university or equivalent program of study.

These educational statistics certainly do not place Thailand within the rank of the most developed nations of the world; professional comparative analysis has determined that they are at the bottom of the third category in a four-level classification of human resource development.[3] Nevertheless, despite the system's still great needs for expansion, improvement, and modernization, Thailand does have a substantial formal education capability. Moreover, the fact that education is even now the primary means of entry into the bureaucratic ruling elite is a source of some optimism about the country's economic, social, and political development potential. For this system, legal access to which is democratic in principle and steadily expanding in reality, makes it increasingly possible for the achievement-oriented of all levels of society to serve the state. In addition, it is preparing them for such service as well as for private life by offering an education which is consciously increasing its westernized components and is steadily being improved in quality. If the Thai bureaucratic ruling class can be increasingly popularized and modernized through the educational system, there is hope for some progress in national development even though mass political participation comes only very slowly. Much will depend in that case, however, on Communist success in political exploitation of the Thai masses and particularly of potentially disaffected groups.

Participatory Capabilities

It should be apparent from previous discussion that the popular participatory capabilities of the Thai polity are in need of major development if there is to be really modern government in Thailand. Military dictatorship, even when well-rooted in national

[3] Frederick Harbison and Charles A. Myers, *Education, Manpower and Economic Growth* (New York: McGraw Hill, 1964), pp. 42, 47.

political traditions of authoritarianism and when reasonably unop-
pressive, is not a stable form of modern government in the long
run. The existing Thai polity is neither sufficiently popularized nor
sufficiently efficient in its solving of society's problems to meet
the criteria of modernity. In fact, mass political participation is
almost nonexistent, political action groups representative of the
key socio-economic sectors of a modern society have not yet
emerged, and regularized structures through which both the general and most specialized publics can effectively articulate their
felt needs and aspirations are absent. All of these shortcomings
become apparent in a review of the respective roles of the country's
various publics. They should not all be blamed on the political
leadership, however, since they are also rooted in the Thai political
heritage and culture.

GENERAL PUBLIC

Thailand's general public (the adult citizenry), to date, has
been characterized most politically by its apathy. This apathy
undoubtedly is the result of a number of factors.

(1) An estimated 85 percent of the population reside in rural
areas and are engaged in cultivation, fishing, hunting, or logging,
while 75 percent live in agricultural households which cultivate two
or more *rai* of land. In the Northeast, the percentage in agricultural households rises to about 88 percent while in the North and
the South it is 79 percent. Only in the Central Plain does it drop to
55 percent because of the great concentration of urban, commercial, and industrial population in the Bangkok-Thonburi capital
city complex (Bangkok had 1,299,528 people in 1960 and its
twin city of Thonburi 403,818). Given the fact that modern mass
communications are limited primarily to a few urban areas and
particularly to the capital area, this extremely high percentage of
population engaged in agricultural activities, many of which are
semisubsistence in character and are performed within a small
village residential pattern, suggests not only economic underde-

velopment in present-day terms but also the existence of an amorphous political majority without much access to modern political communication and political education. Even the urban communities, moreover, are not much more than complexes of villages; after Bangkok and Thonburi, the third biggest municipality is the northern city of Chiengmai with 65,736 people in 1960 (approximately 80,000 now); and there are only 15 municipalities with between 25,000 and 66,000 persons.

(2) The youth of the population also probably constitutes an obstacle to mass political maturity. Almost 70 percent is under the age of 30, almost 82 percent is under the age of 40, and 43 percent is under 15. These statistics suggest that a majority of the population might not be of sufficient legal age to vote even on the basis of the 20 year minimum age now in the new draft constitution.

(3) To this high percentage of young people whose interests would not be political in nature should also be added the estimated 250,000 adult males who are in the Buddhist clergy on either a temporary or permanent basis and so, by both desire and tradition, are withdrawn from worldly pursuits.

(4) Another restriction on mass political participation is probably the literacy level. For although the country claims one of the highest literacy rates in the non-Western world (the 1960 census indicating that 70 percent of the population 10 years of age or older can read and write in some language), this figure undoubtedly becomes lower when it is qualified by two facts: Literacy in the Thai language is necessary to significant national political participation; and many children, once having obtained some literacy in primary school, rarely if ever have an opportunity to employ it because of the lack of a national press or other reading materials throughout the country's villages and hamlets.

(5) Mass political apathy undoubtedly is the nature of Thai political culture and tradition. As noted earlier, that culture and tradition are characterized by limited concern for worldly prob-

lems, belief that improvement in one's condition is to be achieved by ethical rather than material means or social action, respect for hierarchy and authority and belief in the moral basis for inequality of status, preference for individual rather than collective action, and a long history of benevolent but authoritarian political leadership which has been successful in attending to the country's major felt needs and requirements. Such attitudes and traditions, when combined with relative economic and social contentment as well as security of person and property, have provided little basis for active popular participation in the political process. Obviously, therefore, major transformations in the political culture and behavior of the vast majority are required before it can become a politically attentive and active public.

In view of these reasons for political apathy, it is not surprising that, in the eight general elections which have been held for the National Assembly between 1932 and 1958, no more than 40 percent of the limited number of eligible voters have ever actually cast ballots. In fact, in the last general election (December 1957), even though the government campaigned actively to get out the vote in order to legitimatize its assumption of power by coup and members of the Armed Forces were practically marched to the polls, the officially estimated voter turnout was 30 percent of those eligible. Moreover, it was stated at the time that in most elections less than a 30 percent turnout was normal. In the recent (December 1967) municipal elections—the first of these, too, since 1958 —estimates were that, at least in cities like Chiengmai, the turnout was 35 percent to 40 percent of the eligible voters. This first effort at any type of election since 1958, incidentally, was controlled by a prohibition against any discussion of national issues or national leaders. No political parties were involved since they were still illegal, and foreign correspondents noted that members of the existing local "establishment" were the persons running for office.

The basic disinterest of the Thai peasant majority in political action has of course been reflected in the absence of significant pressure groups to promote their special interests. No mass agrarian organizations have been created as representative agencies to articulate claims against government. Similarly, no mass political parties have been established with countrywide organizations rooted in this clearly identifiable majority of the population.

Even before political parties were prohibited and elections for the National Assembly were replaced in 1958 by a completely appointive system, the various political parties which had come and gone since 1932 were actually no more than parliamentary or bureaucratic factions centered about a prominent individual and his small clique of adherents. No real country organizations were ever created although, in 1956 and 1957, the national leadership did attempt to utilize the provincial officials and civil service to provide such a structure for its Seri Mananghasila party. The latter, however, despite this effort, did so poorly in the general elections of February 1957 that it in effect lost the election psychologically, although garnering a small actual majority. Thai political parties, therefore, even when they have existed, have been no more than political clubs usually manipulated by cliques within the ruling elite; two or three of these so-called parties sometimes owing allegiance to the same national leader.

Moreover, at the constituency level, each candidate has been dependent in large measure upon his personal efforts to win election to the National Assembly. He could not easily make appeals to voters in terms of his national party's representation of any broad socio-economic forces or ideology because there was little reality to such claims. Quite often, therefore, parliamentary candidates have run as independents and subsequently have joined a parliamentary party after election to the Assembly. This process has usually benefited the government party since it has had the money and patronage to buy such adherence. After the December 1957 elections, for example, the government party doubled its number of elected seats by mid-January of 1958 through the addition of new parliamentary members recruited from among elected independents and defectors from the major opposition party.

URBAN LABOR

The urban labor force, despite its greater accessibility and involvement in mass communications media, has also been neither politically active nor politically significant. In addition to the pertinent cultural and experiential factors which it shares with the Thai peasantry, its inactivity has probably been the result of several additional factors:

The total number of people in the urban labor force is very small. Not much more than 15 percent of the national population resides in urban areas (50 percent in Bangkok-Thonburi), with approximately one million workers (11 years of age or older) being craftsmen, factory workers, or transportation and communications workers, and approximately 1,200,000 being clerical, sales, or service workers.

This total pool of approximately two and a quarter million urban workers is, in at least one important respect, even more fragmented than are the widely dispersed peasants. For it is divided ethnically between Thai and Chinese, with the latter constituting a majority, particularly at the more skilled levels. Given the relative isolation of the Chinese from Thai politics, their essential cultural autonomy within the society, and their historic cultural preference for collective action through small private groups and organizations based upon family and dialect, this has meant that the Chinese have not been interested in joining the Thai in any common political action.

There is no significant, organized labor movement. Trade unions have been prohibited by the regime since 1958. However, even when they were permitted, the trade unionism which had developed through 1957 reflected the organizational characteristics of the political parties; that is to say, it was largely dependent upon a handful of individual leaders without significant experience in the field. In addition, because of general Thai inexperience with any form of private voluntary association, union members relied on the leadership for all important policy decisions. The latter, for their part, frequently were more interested in the personal political implications of trade unionism than in their economic potentialities. As a result, some leaders actually were dominated by the government while others maneuvered in association with opposition party leaders. From the point of view of the government which assumed power in 1958, this last characteristic was of particular significance because of concern about Chinese loyalty and the extremism of some union leaders.

To the preceding description of unionism may be added the fact that, despite the creation of 136 unions, three legal federations, and one illegal Communist-led federation by the end of 1957, only a relative handful of workers actually were trade union members. This fact is not surprising, however, in view of the limited industrialization of the country and the extent to which private non-agricultural activities are organized into small, family-operated enterprises. An International Bank survey of industrial organizations in 1957, for example, estimated that only about 2 percent of these establishments had more than 50 employees while a 1954 government survey estimated that 28,000 of the 30,500 enterprises in the country had fewer than 10 workers each and that there were no more than 200,000 industrial workers in total. Thai trade unionism, therefore, even when permitted, was very under-developed in all respects. In sum, urban labor, whether organized or unorganized, has had only minimal impact on the political system and has had no real collective economic or political representation.

BUSINESS

Thailand's business community, for its part, has shared, in general, the political weakness which has characterized the peasantry and urban labor. This has been due to several factors:

Business has lacked the organizational basis for maximizing its potential political strength. Reflecting the general absence in the country of effective private cooperative organizations, the few business groups which have emerged to date have been relatively underdeveloped. Moreover, they have suffered from the fragmentation along ethnic lines which has marked nonagricultural labor. Thus, the two general employers' associations have been the Thai and the Chinese Chambers of Commerce, each of which has had its own ethnic constituents and has tended to function autonomously.

The ethnic Thai business group has also suffered from the limited participation of ethnic Thai in nonagricultural activities, the lack of a substantial Thai middle class, and its economic weakness in comparison to the Chinese and foreign business communities in the country.

As for the Chinese group, their economic power has been hobbled, politically, because of their alien image and lack of clear identification with Thai national interests. Thus they have been viewed for the most part by the Thai as economic opportunists without real roots in the country.

All business groups, moreover, have been faced with a Thai national tradition of governmental preeminence. As a result, Thai, Chinese, and foreign business interests have been limited in their political activity primarily to efforts to influence political leaders and government administrators for narrow special-interest objectives. Frequently, in the past, this has meant the buying of goodwill and official sympathy behind the scenes rather than constructive involvement in national economic policy formulation. A contribution to corruption has been more characteristic of past business participation in politics than a contribution to economic development.

While relationships between the government and business generally have been good, therefore, they have not been particularly wholesome. Moreover, the narrow promotion of business interests has not been counterbalanced by private forces representative of mass socio-economic interests. The official elites of the government, backed by the military and police power of the state and without elective roots in the citizenry, have been the bureaucratic arbitrators and virtually autonomous decision-makers in relations between the social, economic, and political structures of society.

OTHER ELEMENTS

The other identifiable elements of Thai society with potentially disparate interests and political needs, the Thai-Lao and Thai-Malay minorities, for instance, or politically dissatisfied professional and intellectual groups, have been equally ineffective in their participation in the political system. On the one hand, they too have lacked effective organization and leadership; on the other hand, they have not in the past felt the achievement of their basic desires sufficiently frustrated by prevailing conditions to drive them to rebellion. Moreover, where influenced by the Thai or a similar political culture, they also have partaken of the general political apathy and tendency to withdraw from conflict rather than to seek it, as well as of the individualism which has limited possibilities for private collective action even in behalf of self-interest.

Thailand, therefore, has a political public, but it is one whose numbers are limited to an estimated maximum of no more than 2 percent of the entire population. It is a political public whose views are influential rather than dominating, and it is one composed primarily of members of the society's elite. Almost all of this elite are either officials of the government, aspirants to government service, or dependent upon the government. Under the contemporary political system, the Thai practice of politics becomes essentially a competition among individuals and cliques within the ruling and bureaucratized elite rather than a process by which the interests and aspirations of the major private groups of the society are articulated and inserted into the political arena—there to compete, be accommodated, be intermingled with official views, and ultimately be rejected or incorporated into public policy.

THE ELITE

It is, then, the Thai elite which almost alone participates actively and effectively in the political process, which makes demands upon the political system in conformity with its interests and aspirations, obtains a meaningful hearing for those demands, and participates in policy decision-making and application. This elite, moreover, given the high degree of integration of political, social, and economic structures, is a true elite whose dominance is established in all three primary subsystems of society. Unlike the British "establishment," however, its preeminence is not subjected to such countervailing forces as the highly organized and effective representation of other major socio-economic groups of society, the existence of a powerful trade union movement, freely competing political parties of varying interest and ideological orientation, and vigorous political democracy. Thailand thus seems to be politically less developed in this regard than even eighteenth-century England or nineteenth-century Prussia, both of which were also governed by nondemocratic oligarchies.

This all-powerful Thai elite has a number of additional outstanding characteristics which must be noted in order to understand the country's particular practice of politics.

The elite is clearly a continuation, with modifications, of the ruling class which had emerged by 1932 under the absolute monarchy. As noted earlier, the 1932 coup was in many ways a logical culmination of the increased bureaucratization and westernization of the Thai state launched by the Chakri kings after 1850 in order to modernize their realm. Concurrent with this development of a modern bureaucracy had been, during the first two decades of the twentieth century, a weakening of royal absolutism and growth of rule by an aristocratic oligarchy. What the 1932 coup did, in effect, was to limit the king's power in law and fact and, simultaneously, reorganize the ruling oligarchy so that, henceforth, it would be dominated not by hereditary aristocrats but by the senior commoner bureaucrats—both civil and military. Thereafter, modifications in the structuring of the elite were along lines which generally continued the process of administrative modernization launched by the earlier regime.

Thus, further use of Western organizational forms and managerial techniques has occurred within the state administration, westernized education of new recruits to the elite as well as in-service training of established bureaucrats has been increased, and some senior businessmen have been directly associated with this revised ruling "establishment." The senior military commanders, moreover, have become the primary source of top national leadership, thereby replacing the aristocratic cliques which had come to dominate under Rama VII immediately prior to the 1932 coup. It is true that some individual royal princes and aristocrats have remained influential while the king himself has slowly regained some measure of political influence if not power. Nevertheless, the bulk of the elite continue to be members of the civil and military bureaucracies, as in the old days.

As a result, the contemporary elite is conservative, bureaucratic, pragmatic, and motivated more by power considerations than by ideology. It has fought no real revolution, evicted no foreign colonial power, and proclaimed its commitment to no utopias. Rather, it has sought to preserve as much of traditional Thailand as possible, adjust what must be adjusted, and otherwise to rule benevolently but profitably for itself.

A second outstanding characteristic is that the elite is hierarchically structured, in conformity with traditional Thai culture; and several distinct levels or "tiers" can be discerned. As analyzed by David Wilson,[4] the top of the pyramid consists of a pool of some ten to fifteen persons actually or potentially capable of dominating the elite, and thereby the country, because of their ability to manipulate the various primary political forces. The pool is composed of senior military commanders, several civilian political leaders who have acquired great reputations through major participation in the 1932 or later coups and in subsequent political maneuvering, and two or three aristocratic figures of reputation who are close to the throne and have not been tarnished by open alignment with cliques defeated in a major coup. Since 1932, no more than six to eight

[4] David Wilson, *Politics in Thailand* (Ithaca, N.Y.: Cornell University Press, 1962), pp. 60–67.

of these figures of power and reputation actually have constituted the inner core of the governing clique, the remainder temporarily playing either supportive or "waiting-in-the-wings" roles.

The second level in the hierarchy is composed of perhaps a thousand senior figures in the various structures which underpin the political system and bind together the society, economy, and state. These are high ranking officers of the Armed Forces (some colonels but usually officers of flag rank), their civilian counterparts in the bureaucracy (special grade civil servants), some politically influential princes, some parliamentary leaders of distinction who have political followings, and some powerful businessmen with close ties to leading personalities of the regime.

At the third level, which constitutes the hierarchy's base, are to be found the educated, interested, and reasonably articulate thousands of persons resident in Bangkok and a few provincial towns who, whether within or without the public bureaucracy, are the Thai equivalent of the middle classes. This politically attentive and sometimes effective public which, together with the first two sectors of the elite comprise no more than 2 percent of the total population, also has been essentially conservative and wedded to the regime, to date. Composed of high school and university graduates and their equivalent, most are middle-level bureaucrats with lesser numbers of professional and white collar personnel, writers and journalists, and businessmen. They are attuned to the political currents and are even willing to be critical, but few are anxious for revolutionary changes.

The entire elite, because of its education and location, is essentially urbanized and partially westernized. These characteristics clearly distinguish it from the rural majority. As a result, although it remains bound to the masses of the population by the common culture and traditions, it also is distinctly different from rural Thailand in much of its behavior and attitudes. It is involved directly in the money and market economy, in the modern national and international communications system, and in the politics of the country. At its highest levels, members are graduates of universities or military academies. It therefore constitutes almost all that is modern in the society. Because of these features, it is also the source of all national leadership in any of the structural systems. There presently are no significant competitive sources from which national leaders may come except those affiliated with the ruling elite. There are no peasant or worker or political leaders resident in Thailand who would represent a challenge to the elite and the regime from outside, other than the Communists.

The Thai elite is self-regenerating in a way which contributes to its near monopolization of power and leadership but also permits achievement-oriented individuals to obtain some career satisfaction regardless of previous social origin or economic condition if they gain higher education. It is not a ruling caste based upon heredity or on feudal land holdings. Therefore, it may be able to accommodate to further modernization and even to some democratization of the state and society without revolutionary action by the masses or violent counterrevolutionary reactions by its own members. In this sense, it is not inevitably an inflexible barrier to development whose forceful removal is an essential prerequisite to progress, a condition which seems to prevail in some other underdeveloped countries of the world.

The ruling elite has been able to absorb its new recruits and provide them with traditionally prestigious and often monetarily rewarding career opportunities. Thailand, therefore, has avoided, to date, the great problem of other countries whose inability to make available culturally satisfying positions to many of its educated has been a major source of danger to the regime. Discontents of this type elsewhere often feel they have no recourse but to promote revolution. However, in Thailand, the steady expansion of the bureaucracy and the military since 1850, and the elimination of aristocratic monopolization of top leadership roles in 1932, has so far stayed in general balance with the growth in the number of educated citizens interested in public employment. For the future, however, it also seems clear that more economic development will have to occur in order for the country both to continue to absorb the mounting numbers of people with advanced education and to absorb them effectively in terms of their new westernized scientific, technological, and economic skills.

The national politics of contemporary Thailand is primarily a competition for power among continuously forming and changing cliques within the ruling elite. It is not a politics based upon competition among modern political parties with countrywide organizations; it is not a politics based upon the articulation of dissensus and conflict of interests among various key socio-economic groups of society; and it has not been a politics based upon challenges to the political system and its adherents from outside the ranks of the politicized. Instead it is the politics of an oligarchy, akin to "palace politics."

Because of this characteristic of the national politics, the in-puts into the political system stem primarily from the heavily bureaucratic elite itself, whose basic level of consensus is high. Thai politics, therefore, is concerned less with conflicts of interest, ideology, and policy objectives than with the distribution of power, authority, and spoils. It is a competition for control among senior personalities and their adherents within the elite. It is a contest, then, among the top dozen or so figures to see which will actually form the inner ruling group and, hence, govern the state and society.

The cliques involved at any time in this contest for power are not totally amorphous and without pattern.[5] Despite the Thai propensity for individual rather than collective action, they are rooted in such basic Thai social relationships as kinship, previous secondary school and university relationships, student-teacher ties, career associations within the bureaucracy, and common respect for a senior personality.

The general outlines of political ideology may sometimes enter into the coalescing of a clique in which the personality around

[5] *Ibid.*, pp. 136–137, and Fred W. Riggs, "Cabinet Politicians in Thailand: A Bureaucratic Elite" (unpublished paper delivered at the September 1962 Annual Meeting of the American Political Science Association, Washington, D.C.)

whom it has formed is a civilian with an established commitment to parliamentary elections (for example, Nai Khuang Aphaiwong) or to economic development (for example, Nai Pridi Phanomyong), or in which the leader is a military figure with nationalistic orientation (for example, Field Marshal Phibulsonggram in the 1930's). Some ideological predilections may also be suggested by the extent to which the organizing personality supports an important role for the throne or desires to restrict it to minimum participation. Willingness to collaborate with one side or another in an international conflict, too, may become a determinant, as was the case in Marshal Phibun's association with the Japanese and Pridi's contact with the Allies in World War II.

Nevertheless, the politics of cliques since 1932 has been more a contest for power for its own sake than a contest between alternative policies. Moreover, it has been a politics in which even loyalty to the leading personality has been less important than political survival, with the result that it has had much of the flavor of that "transformism" which has so characterized modern Italian politics.

In this competition among elitist cliques which has dominated the Thai political system since 1932, the preeminence of the military has led to the significant militarization of the oligarchy.[6] The emergence of the military as the dominant element of the ruling circle actually occurred in several stages. Initially, the 1932 coup was the work of a coalition of bureaucratic groups, both civil and military, with common education abroad and working association under the absolute monarchy. Distinguishable in terms of their junior or senior status under the old regime as well as by their ages, and subsequently joined by some high ranking officials of the monarchy after their initial success, these "promoters" formed the ruling circle which took control of the country. Within a short

---

[6]*Ibid.* See also Morris Janowitz, *The Military in the Political Development of New Nations* (Chicago: University of Chicago Press, 1964), p. 7, who classifies the regime as a "military oligarchy."

period of time, however, the coalition began to fragment as old-line officials who had not actually participated in the coup began to organize against the promoters while the latter split along junior and senior lines.

As a result of this maneuvering during the initial year and a half of the new regime, first the old-line officials and then the senior clique of promoters were eliminated from power in favor of the junior clique, with the young military leaders frequently involved and increasingly more important in deciding the issue. Subsequently, the junior clique itself fragmented, as civilians, army commanders, and naval leaders formed their own cliques. With the suppression by force of an actual military rebellion fomented in October 1933 by a coalition of senior clique promoters, old-line officials, and princes, the ruling circle was restricted to army, navy, and civilian cliques composed primarily of junior members of the original Coup Group. Thereafter, despite periodic alternation between civilians and the military in the top leadership positions, with the chief personalities from all surviving cliques represented to varying extents, the army group steadily acquired ascendancy. Between 1938 and 1944, and from 1947 to the present, military and particularly army domination has been overriding. Thus, the competition for leadership has become primarily a competition among the heads of military cliques, with civilian personalities participating in coalitions and providing support but being unable to reassert their original claim to equal partnership.

In sum, therefore, this militarized and elitist political system provides little if any opportunity for popular participation. Lacking this capability, it is the antithesis of modernity, being semi-traditionalist even in its authoritarianism. It is inevitable that the system will have to be modified in order to survive. Whether the national leadership is itself capable of innovating this modernization ultimately will determine the country's ability to perpetuate that conservative process of adjustment to the new forces of an age which has characterized its political history to date.

Decision-Making Capabilities

The nonmodern character of Thai politics generally is paralleled by the only semimodern nature of the governmental decision-making system. The structures concerned, although superficially Western and parliamentary in form, actually are traditional in their behavioral essence. Moreover, they are characterized more by improvisation than by regularized and long-term solutions to the country's contemporary decision-making requirements. Without additional development, therefore, Thai leadership capabilities will become increasingly inadequate not merely for the promotion of societal modernization, as a whole, but even for the performance of basic government functions. This inadequacy will increase the system's attractiveness as a Communist target.

Under the existing system, the key leadership and decision-making structures center on the throne, the Cabinet, the National Assembly, and the bureaucracy.

THE THRONE

As noted earlier, the Thai monarchy is of great symbolic significance in the promotion of national integration. As a link to Thai history, it is a fundamentally conservative force although not necessarily a reactionary one. In fact, the great and absolute kings of the nineteenth century provided the leadership which made possible the country's controlled modernization during this critical period. Since the termination of royal absolutism in 1932, however, the throne has become an uncertain component in the decision-making complex. For, while the symbolic and ceremonial functions have continued, the king has exercised an intangible influence over the actual course of events. When the original Coup Group seized power with the aid of troops on June 24, 1932, the "promoters" demonstrated their recognition of royal prestige as well as their need to legitimize their action by simultaneously proclaiming the termination of the absolute monarchy and requesting that Rama VII continue to rule as a constitutional monarch. This the King agreed to do in an announcement to the effect that he was granting a provisional constitution drafted by the Coup Group. Subsequently, he designated persons nominated by the Coup Group to form a new Assembly and the latter, through a constitution committee, then formulated the first Permanent Constitution. This document was adopted by the Assembly and proclaimed on December 10, 1932.

Under the Constitution of December 1932, a vaguely British-style parliamentary regime was established and all independent power was removed from the king. However, it was also a regime in which one-half of the Assembly was to be appointed by the Cabinet, rather than be elected, until such time as one-half the eligible voters had received four years of education or ten years had ensued. In effect, then, the decision-making powers of the throne were transferred to the commoner Coup Group. Because of this new form of authoritarianism, Rama VII, who had evidenced some support for the democratization of the monarchy even before the coup, began to press for constitutional revisions to give substance to the remaining royal prerogatives. He argued that since the people did not really control the polity through a meaningful elected Assembly, the throne had a representative role to play in decision-making. Confronted by a rejection of his demands, the King then abdicated on March 2, 1935, and a young royal prince of ten (Ananda Mahidon) ascended the throne under a Council of Regency. The new oligarchy, therefore, had won its contest with the King over royal powers while still preserving the monarchy it required to legitimize its leadership role. Subsequently (1938–1944), the dominant figure in this ruling circle, Field Marshal Phibun, introduced into the system a form of neo-fascism copied from the Axis powers and, in so doing, severely restricted even the ceremonial functions of the throne.

In 1944, Marshal Phibun was overthrown by a civilian clique with the acquiescence of the armed forces he headed. His association with a Japan about to be defeated had made him a liability to Thailand, which faced the need to negotiate for its future independence with the Western powers. With Phibun's overthrow and the return to power of the civilians under Nai Pridi Phanomyong, royal interests were temporarily reasserted by such conservative political leaders as Nai Khuang and Seni Pramoj (the former ambassador to the United States). However, King Ananda was found shot to death on June 9, 1946. This tragedy, which was never satisfactorily explained by Pridi's government, contributed shortly thereafter to Pridi's own overthrow by the Army and the return to power of Marshal Phibun in April 1948. Pridi, an original leader of the civilian members in the 1932 coup, previously had acquired some reputation as a radical because of his 1933 Economic Plan calling for extensive nationalization and the elimination of private enterprise. Many royalists, therefore, suspected him of republican and even Communist aspirations. It is that same Pridi who now resides in Communist China and has had his name associated with the Peking-sponsored Thai Patriotic Front.

The new regime of Marshal Phibun, with various modifications in relationships among dominant cliques and changes in constitution, lasted until September 1957. It continued the earlier Phibun policy of stringently limiting royal activities and participation in decision-making. The new king (Phumiphon Adunyadet), who succeeded his brother to the throne in June 1946, was kept in virtual isolation. Trips abroad or even extensive trips around the country were prevented, and the relationship between the King and his Prime Minister was marked by mutual dislike and distrust. Nevertheless, during 1956 and 1957, there were increasing evidences once again of royal exertion of political influence behind the scenes. For, the pro-royalist civilian group headed by Nai Khuang was still active in the Assembly and the rising military leader, Field Marshal Sarit, also had the reputation of being sympathetic toward the royal family.

When Marshal Sarit actually overthrew the Phibun government in a military coup of September 1957, the King acted with great speed in conferring the Prime Ministership upon Sarit's designee (Marshal Thanom). It was suggested in some political circles that the throne had prior knowledge of the coup but had refused to warn or support Phibun. In any event, since that time, the behind-the-scenes influence of the throne apparently has grown although it probably cannot be called decisive. Relations between the monarchy and the regime have seemed much closer, the contacts more regular and friendly, and the very attractive royal family has traveled extensively both throughout Thailand and the world. Obviously, at a minimum, the new military clique which has been governing since 1958 has viewed this projection of the royal image as an asset, a unifying force within the country as well as a useful international symbol.

Whatever the periodic adjustments in reality since 1932, therefore, the throne, like the Buddhist religion, remains both symbolic of and influential in Thailand. The continued existence of the Thai monarchy, regardless of changes in other structures, appears relatively uncontested despite general agreement that its powers must remain very limited. The royal family thus seems to be evolving along British lines. Political influence, but not decision, is available to it.

THE PRIME MINISTER AND CABINET

While the role of the throne since 1932 generally has been limited to exerting influence rather than exercising decision-making power, and the structures of government have assumed certain Western characteristics, the actual powers of government have not been elaborated within the framework of meaningful constitutionalism. Instead, with the elimination of royal control, the Thai state has become even more oligarchic than it was in the 1920's under Rama VII. Moreover, the fact that a militarized commoner ruling circle has supplanted the traditional princes has made government more dependent upon coercion than was the case from 1850 to 1932. For, in contemporary Thai politics, individual leaders of the major cliques within the governing elite actually seize control by coup d'etat and hold it only so long as no other clique is able to muster sufficient force—primarily military—to oust them. Legitimation is obtained after the fact, through royal appointment to the major ministerial offices of the state. No real discretion in this legalization of coups is allowed the monarch.

The nature of this relationship between the throne and a Coup Group is made very clear in the Interim Constitution of 1959, under which the country presently is being governed. In that document, officially proclaimed by the King after Marshal Sarit had seized power in his own name from Marshal Thanom, his senior subordinate military commander (whom Sarit previously had sponsored for the Prime Ministership), one finds the following:

> His Majesty King Phumiphon Adunyadet is graciously pleased to make known that
> Whereas the Leader of the Revolutionary Party, after the successful seizure of power on October 20, B.E. 2501, has represented to him that the abrogation of the Constitution of the Kingdom of Thailand, B.E. 2475 as amended in B.E. 2495, was actuated by the desire to acquire an appropriate Constitution and to achieve greater improvements in the national administration than would have been feasible under the former Constitution:
> And whereas to attain this end, it is deemed expedient to set up a Constituent Assembly composed of qualified members to draft a new Constitution to meet the present need and conditions:
> His Majesty the King, approving these resolves and in order to give effect to the proposals of the Leader of the Revolutionary Party, hereby graciously commands that the following provisions be promulgated and enforced as the Constitution of the Kingdom of Thailand pending the Constitution to be drafted by the Constituent Assembly:—

Among other provisions, the new Interim Constitution then goes on to note that the King appoints the Prime Minister and the Council of Ministers, who are "responsible for the national administration"; that the "Council of Ministers exercises the executive power . . . in the name of the King"; that "every law, Royal Prescript, and Royal Command relating to affairs of State shall be countersigned by the Prime Minister or a Minister"; that the King will appoint all 240 members of the Constituent Assembly; that the Prime Minister can, by Council resolution, legally engage in all necessary actions to suppress threats to "national security" and "law and order"; and that "Before the Council of Ministers is formed, the Leader of the Revolutionary Party shall discharge the duties of the Council of Ministers and the Prime Minister." This constitutional document is "Countersigned by Field Marshal Sarit Thanarat, Leader of the Revolutionary Party."

The contemporary Thai ministerial positions, therefore, are not modern in either democratic or totalitarian terms. They resemble those in Western cabinet systems only in their formal executive definition, for they lack democratic representative substance. They do not mirror the substantive political characteristics of modern totalitarian dictatorship, either, since they are not rooted in the mass single parties and corporative structures of fascism or of communism's "people's democracy." As a result the decision-making system is essentially one of traditional authoritarianism even though the king is limited in power, a commoner instead of an aristocratic oligarchy runs the state, and the official positions held are modern in title.

The self-selected Council of Ministers (Cabinet) does, however, constitute the locus of actual leadership and decision-making power. It is the primary official agency through which authoritative national leadership is exercised. Sitting in the Cabinet, the polity's senior oligarchs formulate policy, devise law, direct and coordinate administration, and engage in whatever degree of promotion of national cohesion and societal development they so wish. There is no real separation of governmental powers in the system and there is no effective competition for leadership from outside the Cabinet until such time as a new coup occurs. Power and authority, executive and legislative, thus are fused in the persons of the chief members of the ruling clique, who occupy simultaneously the key Cabinet posts and the informal leadership positions of the Coup Group.

The traditional basis for the Cabinet is to be found in the ministerial offices which evolved under the old monarchy.[7] In the early period of the Chakri kingdom, there were two senior ministers, one of whom served as the equivalent of a viceroy for the North and the other for the South. In addition to these territorially based positions, there were four ordinary ministers with functional responsibilities (City, Palace, Fields, and Treasury). All, like the rest of the bureaucracy, were completely dependent upon royal authority for the conduct of their individual offices, and they had no collective roles to perform.

From 1851 to 1932, however, Thai government underwent steady modernization designed to westernize it through further administrative centralization, rationalization, and specialization. As a result, more clearly defined and modern functional ministries were created and the problem of administrative coordination was dealt with by the establishment of a Council of Ministers which held regular meetings. Final decision, however, remained with the king, who served as head of the Council and thereby acted as his own prime minister. When Rama VII ascended to the throne in 1925, he also created a Supreme State Council composed of senior royal princes. They did not necessarily hold ministerial posts, but advised the king on policy matters which he would be discussing with the Cabinet. By creating the State Council, Rama VII thus provided the princely ruling circle with a special collective role in policy formulation and governmental supervision while leaving to the regular Council of Ministers the function of linking the throne to the state administration, over which it still maintained direct control. After 1932, however, the Supreme State Council became a Privy Council of royal advisors while the Cabinet (Council of Ministers) has emerged as the dominant organ of government.

Since 1958, twelve ministries have been represented in the Cabinet by their ministers, with the total membership more than doubled by the addition of various deputy ministers and deputy

[7] See Wilson, pp. 144–149.

prime ministers. Recently, these ministries have been Foreign Affairs, Defense, Interior, Finance, Justice, Industry, Agriculture, Cooperatives, Education, Economic Affairs, Communications, and Public Health. Previous constitutions stipulated varying numbers of ministers ranging from 14 to 28. (The new draft constitution lists 15 to 25.) Under Thai practice, all ministers are Cabinet members, and there is no British-type distinction between the members of the Cabinet as a senior group and the other ministers. Normally, the leader of the victorious clique assumes the Prime Ministership and perhaps one or two additional ministerial posts. The remainder of the positions are filled either by associated or at least cooperative figures of importance (military commanders, political figures, or men of personal prestige) or by relatively nonpolitical experts with technical skills. In the new draft constitution, the ministers also will not be allowed to be members of parliament, although they will be permitted to participate in its debates and discussions. By and large, all ministers must be judged loyal or at least not antagonistic to the ruling clique. Administrative competence is also viewed as desirable, although this criterion appears to be applied most to the expert members since senior military commanders often obtain ministries in fields which are greatly removed from their professional qualifications. In the latter case, it is common for a senior civilian bureaucrat to serve as deputy minister. It is, then, on the compliant administrative experts that each government relies for much of its administrative effectiveness.

While the ruling clique customarily assumes such key official posts as the Prime Ministership and the Ministries of Defense and Interior plus several other ministries, its membership is not identical to that of the Cabinet because of the additional ministers and deputies previously referred to. As a result, the Coup Group (whatever its specific label) may also meet regularly on an extra-legal basis either to formulate national policy or to consider possible challenges to its control of the country. Such meetings may even be publicized in the Bangkok newspapers. Subsequently, those members of the group who hold ministerial positions will participate in an official Cabinet meeting and transmit the wishes of the ruling clique. So long as the latter is in control, there is no question about Cabinet implementation of its extra-legal decisions. In this way, the traditional royal political irresponsibility is perpetuated by the new commoner rulers.

It is also important to recognize, however, that—unlike the absolute kings—the governors of contemporary Thailand cannot stay in power or govern effectively without reference to the broader elite of which they are a part. Although they are politically irresponsible as far as the masses of society are concerned, they do have constituencies within the elite whose support they require. Thus, the officer corps of the Armed Forces must be kept aligned, the senior career civilian bureaucrats (the higher civil service) must remain compliant, individual nonbureaucratic political leaders of prominence who have supporters in the Assembly or throughout the small political public must be placated, and major business interests must be accommodated. Each individual minister, moreover, becomes responsible for representing the special interests of his particular sector of the bureaucracy within the Cabinet and Coup Group. Policy formulation, as a result, does require that conflicting claims be accommodated, where possible; that some demands be given priority over others; and that maximum political consensus be maintained in the interests of political stability. However, the claims involved derive primarily from within the ruling elite (that 1 to 2 percent of the population previously identified), which means that claims come mainly from within the civil and military bureaucracies of the political system itself. This bureaucratization of Thai politics is reflected in the degree to which most Cabinet ministers have had long years of prior public administrative service. Fred W. Riggs has identified 75 percent of all Cabinet ministers from 1932 to 1958 as military or civil career officials and only 5 percent as nonbureaucrats, with the remainder being of indeterminate backgrounds. Of the 160 bureaucrats out of a total of 212 ministers during this period, 88 were senior civil servants and 72 senior military officers.[8]

In contemporary Thailand, therefore, the senior leadership roles are filled by the chiefs of bureaucratized cliques within the ruling class who are under no real obligation to concern themselves with parliamentary majorities. Authority is theirs because they had the power to impose themselves in a competition with other similar cliques. Despite constitutional statements there is no political necessity for, or tradition in behalf of, executive responsibility to the legislature—even a legislature representative of an oligarchy. Whatever political responsibility exists, then, is to the civil and military bureaucracies which are the primary constituencies. There are no effective counterweights either within the polity or the society to this executive monopolization of state decision-making.

THE NATIONAL ASSEMBLY

Pre-1932 Thai experience with legislative bodies was limited primarily to the quasi-legislative Council of State created by Rama V in 1874 and subsequently transformed in 1894 into an Assembly of State Councilors. These bodies, whose legislative recommendations to the absolute monarchy were subject both to royal and ministerial veto, had appointed members drawn from the senior bureaucracy. After 1907, however, they were not utilized by Rama VI, and Rama VII substituted his princely Supreme State Council as an advisory body. Contemporary Thailand, therefore, has had virtually no experience either with political institutions which represented elements of society other than the bureaucracy (civil and military) or with real legislative bodies. The national political culture, even as modified since 1850, clearly defines political leadership in executive rather than in legislative terms.

Experience acquired in the operation of a legislature since

[8] See Riggs.

1932 has been uneven and relatively unimpressive. The membership of the first Assembly which met in June 1932 under the initial
Provisional Constitution was selected by the Coup Group from
among its own supporters. Under the Permanent Constitution
promulgated in December 1932 (which lasted until May 1946),
an equal number of assemblymen were indirectly elected but in
such fashion that the control of the Coup Group was not jeopard-
ized. The introduction of direct election for assemblymen in the
November 1937 general elections did not enhance legislative
power and, in fact, the Assembly actually began a steady decline
with the concurrent assumption of the Prime Ministership by Field
Marshal Phibun. It was only in 1944, with Phibun in political
difficulty because of impending Japanese defeat and discontent at
home, therefore, that the Assembly actually succeeded in producing a real change of government through the rejection of major
government bills. In two previous government resignations because of Assembly votes (1934 and 1937), the result had been
little more than a reshuffling of the Cabinet. In 1944, however,
Pridi and Khuang rallied their respective cliques and Phibun was
induced to resign. Even then, however, this change in prime ministers was not so much a victory for parliamentary authority as it
was a product of international necessity, to which both civil and
military bureaucracies responded.

From 1944 through 1947, the Pridi liberals and Khuang
royalists continued to manifest their strength and engage in active
political maneuvering within the legislative arena. Their dominance, in conjunction with the emergence of the legislature as an
active participant in the decision-making process, however, was a
temporary postwar phenomenon dependent upon political confu-
sion within the Armed Forces. During this brief period, Pridi did
attempt to perpetuate the legislature's new role by formulating
another so-called Permanent Constitution. It established a two-
house legislature, replacing appointive members with persons
chosen by indirect election to sit in an upper chamber. The lower
chamber was directly elected. Nevertheless, despite this manifes-

tation by Pridi of a greater sympathy for European parliamentar-
ianism than was true of the military, he also demonstrated the
Thai politician's preoccupation with gaining and retaining power
(rather than with democracy) by making certain that almost all
of his supporters were elected to the upper house.

Unfortunately, this limited experimentation with parliamentary
politics, which included the development of a number of active
political "parties" within the legislature (but without a popular
base), was brought to an end by the reassertion of military su-
premacy in 1947. First, the military ousted Pridi in a coup of
November 1947 and established Khuang as a transitional Prime
Minister. Subsequently, it forced his resignation in favor of Marshal Phibun in April 1948. All of these changes were imposed
without reference to the elected Assembly or to the wishes of its
majority. A new Provisional Constitution was proclaimed in November 1947 at the time of the coup, and still another Permanent
Constitution followed in March 1949. During this two-year period,
in which Phibun was consolidating his power, the upper house
was again made appointive and was employed to assure the government of majority control of the Assembly. By 1951, therefore,
the military was able to restore the original tutelage arrangement
of 1932 under which half of a single chamber was appointed; and,
in February 1952, Thailand returned officially to a revised version of the 1932 Permanent Constitution.

This effective harnessing of the Assembly after 1951 was
somewhat weakened during the period from 1955 to 1959 by the
mounting fragmentation of the ruling Coup Group into three military cliques: those of Marshal Phibun, Marshal Sarit, and Police
General Phao. As a result, legislative debate increased once more
and new "parties" began to vocalize criticism of the government.
However, since no real national parties had ever developed, this
activity actually involved little more than the partial transfer to
the parliamentary arena of the political maneuvering among elitist
cliques of the ruling circle. It is true that, in the midst of this
struggle among the oligarchs, some vaguely leftist parliamentary

members from the depressed Northeast did emerge and attempt to introduce a measure of economic, social, and foreign policy debate into Thai politics. Limited efforts were also made to appeal to the urban workers of Bangkok in similar terms. Nevertheless, even this relatively novel introduction of substantive policy questions into Thai political discussion did not change the fact that transfers in power still depended upon military coups d'etat, not parliamentary votes of confidence.

In the face of both leftist and monarchist criticism of the regime within the Assembly, and the even more serious bid for power by Sarit's army clique, Phibun and Phao were forced into a defensive alliance. However, while the Prime Minister attempted to retain his position mainly by balancing off Phao and Sarit, the ambitious police general seemed to sense that some modernization of the political process was necessary if for no other reason than to provide a broader base from which he himself eventually could gain the Prime Ministership. General Phao also was aware that increasing appeals to a larger political public both by non-Communist leftists and by Chinese Communist sponsored activists could be met more effectively if he could link popular support to the para-military police forces under his command. Marshal Phibun, for his part, was willing to go along with limited political experimentation of this type after a visit to the United States and Europe impressed upon him the power of their popularly elected leaders.

However, the Phibun-Phao effort was frustrated by the inability of their Seri Mananghasila party to gain an overwhelming victory in the general election of February 1957 despite extensive manipulation. The new Assembly engaged in even more active and critical debate while Bangkok students took to the streets to protest the reputed falsification of election returns. As a result, Marshal Sarit and the army, which he had come to control as commander-in-chief, were presented with an opportunity to seize power in the name of political honesty and popular will. Successful coups were undertaken first in September 1957 (overthrowing

Phibun and Phao) and then in October 1958—the latter terminating the existing Constitution, dissolving the Assembly, and then reconstituting it on a completely appointive basis as a Constituent Assembly. It was then assigned the responsibility, at some unspecified time in the future, to produce yet another "permanent" constitution. Thailand since 1958, therefore, has functioned without any nationally elected body and essentially as a military dictatorship. Under the new draft constitution, two houses are again specified for parliament with the Senate to be appointed by the King (which is to say, the government) and the House of Representatives to be elected. This should once more, as in the past, assure the government of a parliamentary majority and reasonably effective control over the legislative process.

What this brief summary of the trials and tribulations of the Thai national legislature obviously indicates is the extent to which that body is underdeveloped and without established authority as an effective participant in the decision-making process. The status of the legislature is not surprising, of course, in view of its lack of rooting in Thai political culture and tradition. It is even less surprising in the face of that bureaucratization of Thai politics previously discussed. However, while effective legislatures are not essential to effective government in societies whose entire tradition is one of authoritarian executive leadership, their absence certainly prevents the development of political democracy. Moreover, in a transitional period, it also weakens the claim to legitimacy of a regime whose supreme leaders have only tenuous traditional claims to the roles which they now fill. Unquestionably, therefore, slowly emerging pressures within Thailand for broader popular participation in the political system eventually will force the establishment not only of parties to replace the existing cliques but of a politics which, although possibly not democratic in Western terms, will nevertheless require a more meaningful legislative arena for some of its expression. The existing decision-making system is too unstable and irrational (in modern terms) to be considered permanent. It is also oriented more toward the survival in power of its key figures than to long-term national problem-solving and development.

It is certainly not fair or sensible to expect that today's Thailand should have a fully functioning, Western-style democratic political system. The nation's political history and culture provide no basis for it. After all, most countries throughout all of human history have had types of political systems which would not qualify as democratic in contemporary Western terms. One cannot ignore the fact that the existing systems of Western Europe and North America really became democratized only from the middle of the nineteenth century on and that many continental European states have been struggling to establish and maintain successful democracies almost down to the present day. One certainly cannot demand more of a completely Asian society than of a Germany, a France, or an Italy. On the other hand, it is possible to observe that, regardless of historic era or of political ideology, a country's survival requires "good" government, meaning effective, problem-solving government. In the present age it must also be popular government with meaningful mass involvements.

CHAPTER V

❧

The Thai
Administrative System

In analyzing Thai public administrative capabilities for the performance both of basic and of developmental functions, several interrelated questions are of paramount importance: How modern is the operative definition of administrative roles and functions? How effectively is the public administrative system structured? What are the modernization needs of Thai public administration itself? Obviously, since all government depends heavily on its administrative system both as part of its decision-making apparatus and in order to carry out those decisions, the promotion of Thai national security and of development requires effective public administration.

Roles and Functions

The contemporary Thai public administrative system performs a number of identifiable roles within the polity and the society. Some of these roles definitely contribute significantly both to governmental effectiveness and to societal stability. Others, however, actually constitute obstacles to national development because their basic purposes run contrary to the requirements for modernization. These interacting roles may be categorized as follows: (1) major participation through senior bureaucrats, especially military ones, in national policy-making and domination of provincial and local decision-making; (2) linking of Thai government to the traditional national culture; (3) provision of public employment for educated and ambitious Thai as well as for a major proportion of the nonagricultural work force; (4) introduction into Thai government of some modern, foreign (currently Western) administrative forms and techniques; (5) performance of a number of administrative functions essential to governmental effectiveness and stability.

POLITICAL-ADMINISTRATIVE RELATIONSHIPS

The general nature of the relationship between the political and administrative components of the Thai polity has already been suggested by the description of Thai politics as elitist, militarized, and bureaucratized.[1] This means, in effect, that one sector of the public administrative system—the military bureaucracy—dominates the polity in association with a compliant and participating civil bureaucracy. Both, moreover, constitute the core of the nation's governing elite as well as of its political public. Thailand, therefore, lacks a major characteristic of political modernity (dem-

---

[1] An excellent discussion of the Thai bureaucracy is provided by William J. Siffin, in "The Thai Bureaucracy" (unpublished paper presented at the September 1961 Annual Meeting of the American Political Science Association, St. Louis, Missouri). See also Siffin, *The Thai Bureaucracy: Institutional Change and Development* (Honolulu: East-West Center Press, 1966); Daniel Wit, *Labor Law and Practice in Thailand* (Washington, D.C.: U.S. Department of Labor, Bureau of Labor Statistics Report No. 267, March 1964), Part I, pp. 5–6, 28–29, and 29–32; M. Ladd Thomas, "Thai Public Administration," *The New Zealand Journal of Public Administration*, XXV, No. 1 (September 1961), 13–33; Siffin, "The Civil Service of the Kingdom of Thailand," *International Review of Administrative Sciences*, XXVI, No. 3 (1960), 255–268; Edgar Shor, "The Thai Bureaucracy," *Administrative Sciences Quarterly*, V, No. 1 (June 1960), 66–86; and Fred W. Riggs, *Thailand: The Modernization of a Bureaucratic Polity* (Honolulu: East-West Center Press, 1966).

ocratic or totalitarian): The public administrative system is not subordinated to external political direction and control. Instead, the country's political structures are less developed and modernized than its administrative structures, with the result that the polity is dominated by its administrative subsystem. Such bureaucratized government manifests many long-term weaknesses as well as several short-term strengths.

On the positive side, this effective linking of the political and administrative, with senior military administrators governing the state and senior civilian administrators participating as Cabinet members and deputy ministers, permits government to implement policy decisions with a minimum of external political interference. Government, therefore, is reasonably effective and stable in minimal terms, although authoritarian. Even the military coups d'etat are essentially palace revolutions within the ruling elite which do not affect the basic politico-administrative relationships: The civilian bureaucracy merely transfers its allegiance to the new military oligarchs with little evidence of tension or of serious concern. As long as the general public remains politically apathetic, no organized socio-economic groups of consequence challenge this form of government, and the king continues to legitimize the regime in popular eyes, the country is an island of stability within an otherwise extremely turbulent Southeast Asian sea. As already remarked, however, the future permanency or attractiveness of these relationships is questionable.

On the negative side of the contemporary politico-administrative relationship, one can identify several significant liabilities. For one thing, the elitist character of government in both its political and administrative aspects produces a conservatism and commitment to the status quo which probably is detrimental to long-term stability in a revolutionary era from which Thailand cannot remain completely isolated. The present bureaucratization of the polity may create short-term stability but it is antagonistic to development, which requires the primacy of the "political."

A second drawback in the existing pattern of relationships is that of excessive political intervention for nonpolicy reasons in the operation of the administrative system. In contemporary Thailand, political considerations which reflect the interests of the ruling military oligarchy often have been more important than rational government programs, effectiveness in problem-solving, or administrative efficiency. Since Thai politics is characterized by an elitist competition for power and spoils unrelated to substantive policy considerations, the victorious clique seeks administrative benefits in the form of jobs for the faithful and for friends. Recruitment, placement, and promotion rules are waived or even violated by Cabinet and ministerial action to accomplish this end, particularly in the case of senior administrative positions under the career service (which includes all classified civil service positions through the undersecretaries). Moreover, in the past when there were general elections, the ruling group has been prone to utilize the bureaucracy in behalf of its favored parties and candidates. Thus, while it is accurate to note that the polity is bureaucratized and relatively uncontrolled by the general citizenry, it is also true that civil administration is extensively manipulated by its military masters, who demand of it chiefly compliance, subservience, and the ability to perform basic functions sufficiently well to prevent difficulties for the regime. Creative, innovative, and developmental administration has been assigned a very low priority in the past.

ADMINISTRATION AND TRADITIONALISM

In addition to its major role in policy-making, a second role performed by the administrative system has been to root government as firmly as possible in the traditional culture. This, too, makes development difficult even though it contributes significantly to the country's stability. It has meant that, despite the bureaucracy's willingness to borrow some laws and administrative techniques from abroad, its primary concern has been not developmental change but the preservation of the state and society—and its own position in them—in terms which perpetuate the status quo as much as possible. Therefore, it has actively promoted only those modifications and adjustments in the system judged essential to accomplish these conservative objectives.

Criticisms of the government's previous economic development efforts are very much to the point in this respect. As remarked earlier, Thai economic growth from 1850 to 1950 was achieved largely without government assistance. While this can be viewed favorably in terms of official willingness to allow private enterprise to bear primary responsibility for the economy, it loses a measure of this virtue when it is also recalled that much more could have been done at least to provide private enterprise with that social overhead capital—transportation, communication, resource conservation, modern banking, power, irrigation and water control—essential to its efforts. Although some important investments of this sort were made in the economy by government, the national need was only partially met. Old Siam, emerging from traditionalism in the same historic era as Japan, obviously did not accomplish in modernization and development what the Japanese accomplished.

Since 1950 and particularly since 1958, it is true, the Thai government consciously has done more to promote economic development than it did earlier. Government does provide, now, about one-third of the total investment in the economy, and there has been an important expansion in overhead capital facilities. Nevertheless, it still remains true that the promotion of economic development has not been the primary preoccupation of the bureaucratized government. It has remained excessively concerned with the preservation of its traditional position in the society and the specific prerogatives of its own personnel. The pursuit of power within the ruling elite is still the primary preoccupation. The guiding attitude toward economic development remains one of doing chiefly what must be done to preserve the regime rather than one of vigorous performance of the development function as in the case of the Japanese. The emphasis continues to be on relatively limited and carefully controlled development in the interest of preserving stability by avoiding rapid societal transformation. This is true not only in regard to the economy, but also in regard to the social system. While the importance of stability cannot be denied, there must also be more realization of the fact that it can only be maintained in an increasingly dynamic context through progressive changes which improve national problem-solving capabilities.

Within the government and bureaucracy itself, moreover, there is still an excessive preoccupation with traditionalist objectives. For, although cultural flexibility sufficient to introduce some westernized changes has been demonstrated, traditional Thai values and behavioral patterns continue to predominate. As a result, there is only limited emphasis on substantive program accomplishment, on performance efficiency, and on productivity. The Thai public administrative system, internally, remains oriented primarily toward stability and self-preservation in traditional value terms. The Western administrative forms and regulations are not really applied for Western purposes. Traditional cultural attitudes toward the definition of "accomplishment" have not yet been replaced by achievement criteria.

PUBLIC EMPLOYMENT

The provision of public employment for educated and ambitious Thai as well as for a large percentage of the nonagricultural work force is a third major characteristic and function of the Thai public administrative system. Once again, it is a function whose successful performance has contributed significantly to national stability but, generally, at the expense of development. For example, official 1960 census statistics list a total of 489,452 persons employed by the government in the following categories:

128

	GOVERNMENT	TOTAL LABOR FORCE
Professional, technical, and related workers	128,832	173,960
Administrative, executive, and managerial	8,668	26,191
Clerical	122,765	154,303
Sales	886	735,457
Farmers, fishermen, loggers, hunters, etc.	2,845	11,332,489
Miners, quarrymen, etc.	508	26,255
Transport and communications	21,298	144,610
Craftsmen, production process, and laborers	74,725	806,205
Service, sport, and recreation	61,980	273,375
Workers unclassified by occupation	66,945	99,259
TOTAL	489,452	13,772,104

These figures indicate that the government employs approximately 25 percent of the nonagricultural work force and that, if the self-employed are excluded, the total probably is about one-third of all nonagricultural wage earners. The Thai government, therefore, is the largest employer of nontraditional labor. But, as remarked above, it is also an employer which is not overwhelmingly committed either to its own internal modernization or to major societal modernization.

Other official Thai statistics indicate that, as of 1961, there were 221,171 regular national civil servants, 150,000 temporary government employees, 10,000 municipal employees, and approximately 53,000 commune and village officials, apart from employees of the estimated 130 government-owned or -controlled enterprises. Of the 221,171 regular officials, however, 112,605 were in the Ministry of Education, and 89,000 of these were schoolteachers actually under the jurisdiction of a teacher's association rather than the national Civil Service Commission. Moreover, an estimated 20 percent of the regular civil servants were police. To these totals of public employees can be added an estimated 130,000 members of the Armed Forces, most of whom were conscripts serving for two years. There was also a Volunteer Defense Corps of about 120,000 designed to assist the police to maintain public order in an emergency. Since 1963, this corps has been training under army supervision. Based on these statistics, the regular civil service amounts to about 1 percent of the population, and the total public service, including career military officials, is probably about 2 percent. Most significantly, these percentages duplicate those for the ruling class of the country.

The fact that the Thai government is the major employer of labor in the modern sector of the economy obviously has contributed greatly to the avoidance of large-scale urban unemployment. In fact, the 1960 census lists the extremely low figure of 0.5 percent of the total economically active population as being unemployed. This fact undoubtedly has served to reduce popular pressures for major economic reforms and thereby has contributed to stability and complacency. The concurrent fact that underemployment is great is not particularly dangerous, apparently. Most underemployment is in the rural areas, where much of the population is economically inactive between planting and harvesting cycles. But this is a traditional feature of Thai cultivation, and there is no significant rural starvation in this land of relative agricultural plenty. Other sources of underemployment are such nonagricultural but seasonal workers as construction workers, the millions of "own account" or self-employed workers (4,084,792), and the even larger number of unpaid family workers on the farms and in the cottage industries (7,982,836). However, these persons, too, are not economically destitute in their own eyes and are able to get along without making demands upon government. To date, therefore, although the Thai government does not employ an abnormally large proportion of the total population, it does employ a great percentage of those nonagricultural workers who otherwise might be unemployed and hence a threat to societal stability. Moreover, it provides them with sufficient job satisfaction to give them a vested interest in the regime.

The regular civil service or official bureaucracy, as previously noted, is a particularly significant source of employment. Traditionally, it is the primary career outlet for most ambitious and educated Thai citizens. Since a sufficiently modern private enterprise economy does not yet exist to absorb them, and the cultural emphasis on government employment rather than on private commercial and industrial employment has not changed very much, this continues to be the case. Nevertheless, despite the great contribution to stability which results from the conscious absorption of the educated elite into the public service, it is also clear that the government is not going to be able to continue to absorb the same percentage of the urban work force indefinitely. The educational system, responding to sizeable population growth, increasingly will produce more people than the government can properly add to its rolls, while the numbers of unskilled urban laborers also will increase. Government income, moreover, is so inadequate even now that the salaries and wages provided are very low and bear a direct relationship to the amount of corruption found in the public service. Yet, about 70 percent of the annual national budget goes to pay civil service salaries, alone. Private enterprise, therefore, must expand to absorb anticipated increases in the work force.

Furthermore, the fact that the government has operated at least 130 different public enterprises in its absorption of much of this urban work force may have kept down the size of unemployment rolls but, simultaneously, it has done little for the nations' productive capacity. Instead, men, money, and materiel have been utilized so inefficiently in most cases that professional analysts of the economy such as the 1958 International Bank mission recommended the dismantling of most of these enterprises. In the long run, it is felt, national economic development will be promoted best by reducing this form of government participation in the economy and stimulating private enterprise in accordance with national resources and capabilities.

PUBLIC ADMINISTRATION AS MODERNIZER

The fact that the Thai public administrative system is heavily oriented toward the performance of functions of conservation and stability does not mean that it has been inflexibly reactionary. As discussed earlier, its modernization during the latter part of the nineteenth and first two decades of the twentieth centuries constituted the heart of royal efforts to bring Siam abreast of more developed countries. Similarly, since 1932, the system has been subjected to various structural reforms designed to improve its modernity and efficiency. During both periods, as well as in earlier centuries, the Thai leadership was demonstrating its historic willingness selectively to borrow and adapt from foreign sources those techniques, laws, and even programs which suited its purposes and its interpretation of national objectives. The result, as will be noted in subsequent discussion of public administrative structures, has been an intermingling of the traditional and the modern.

Nevertheless, even in this aspect of society, which has consciously been subjected to modernizing influences, analysis reveals that modernization is often more superficial than substantive. Many of the imported administrative techniques have been used in relatively traditional ways and for traditional objectives. Like some of the modern Western laws incorporated into the system (e.g., in the areas of social welfare, labor law, labor relations, and labor administration), little has actually been done to implement these paper innovations. Thus, although the administrative system does provide evidences of modernization, the basic bureaucratic preoccupation with conservation, stability, and self-interest, plus the absence of modern political leadership to provide the necessary goals, stimulation, direction, and supervision, seriously restricts the development process. The Thai experience raises the fundamental question: How far can traditional, bureaucratized, oligarchical systems really go in self-reform? Without such self-reform, they obviously do not have the capabilities to reform, modernize, and develop their societies.

ADMINISTRATIVE PERFORMANCE

The conservative and semitraditionalist character of the Thai public administrative system, as just described, certainly has not produced governmental chaos. A country capable of engaging in some 700 years of independent national existence obviously must be solving at least its basic governmental problems. This, in fact, has been the case. For, although the polity cannot be called "modern" and clearly committed to its own or the nation's rapid development, it has been possessed of administrative capabilities sufficient to meet many important needs. Government and its administrative apparatus have been able to preserve national security, to date. Internal law and order have been reasonably well maintained. Various legal and administrative support services have been provided the masses of the population in their agricultural activities; and, in recent years, some also have been extended to urban economic enterprise as well. An expanding educational system, improved public health conditions, and a reasonably "hard" currency constitute additional accomplishments.

Thai government, therefore, does have a record of independent achievement. It has performed enough basic functions sufficiently well over a long period of time to keep its people relatively happy and complacent. There have been no revolutions and no great popular turmoil. This cannot be overlooked. Nevertheless, it is not the Thai past but the Thai future that is in question. That future, it appears to this writer, increasingly will be placed in serious jeopardy unless public administrative capabilities are modernized and further developed to the point where they can satisfactorily help to solve the new national problems appearing on the horizon. Such administrative development as a prerequisite to societal development, however, must in turn be harnessed to even greater political development. For, without political development, Thailand will probably continue to expand its administrative structures and bureaucracy within existing goal and behavior patterns; that is, it will continue to perform roles and functions which are not primarily developmental in substance. As Professor William J. Siffin has observed in regard to Thai public administration, "[in substantive terms] not much development has taken place in Thailand since the Chakri Reformation [nineteenth century]. . . . In terms of another criterion—survival—the Thai system has sufficed." [2]

Administrative Structures

GENERAL PATTERN

In the formal structuring of the public administrative system, supreme leadership is vested in the Prime Minister and Cabinet, who provide general administrative supervision and control, arbitrate conflicting bureaucratic interest claims and jurisdictional disputes, and otherwise make major administrative policy decisions. Excessive centralization and the upward transfer of responsibility for administrative decisions, based upon fear of making "bad" decisions which might displease superiors, is characteristically so great, however, that the Prime Minister and Cabinet are unnecessarily overburdened by their administrative role. This, in turn, reduces the amount of time available to them for a serious consideration of national policy matters. Overcentralization of administrative decision-making, therefore, is a serious general weakness whose causes are both political (the nature of the regime) and cultural.

The Prime Minister is aided by the Office of the President of the Council of Ministers, which contains twenty-three administrative units. Roughly comparable to the Executive Office of the President of the United States, this office which reports directly to the Prime Minister, includes such important administrative agencies as the Civil Service Commission, the National Economic Development Board, the Central Intelligence Agency, the Adminis-

[2] Siffin, *The Thai Bureaucracy: Institutional Change and Development,* pp. 253–254.

tration Inspection Department, the Public Relations Department, and the Budget Office. It is headed by a Secretary-General, who serves as the Prime Minister's administrative assistant and has become the major instrument through which the Prime Minister controls and supervises the national administrative system. Its reorganization since 1958, which also has led to the tightening of its lines of responsibility to the Prime Minister (as distinguished from the Cabinet), has contributed significantly to the enhancement of that officer's preeminence and effectiveness.

Directly under the Office of the President of the Council of Ministers are twelve ministries whose heads, the ministers and deputy ministers, constitute the Cabinet. With the development of the Office of the President of the Council, the Cabinet's collective functions of administrative coordination, control, and supervision have tended to be assumed increasingly by that office. This tendency has been facilitated, too, by the extent to which the ministries function as semiautonomous sub-bureaucracies within the system and impose upon their ministers the obligation of promoting their ministries' special interests and programs. The result has been the use of the Cabinet, meeting once or twice a week, primarily as a senior committee for the reconciliation and compromising of administrative differences as well as for the formulation of national policy.

The twelve ministries are Agriculture, Communications, Cooperatives, Defence, Economic Affairs, Education, Finance, Foreign Affairs, Industry, Interior, Justice, and Public Health. Their general organizational structure is similar and follows a relatively conventional Western pattern. The minister, a political appointee, serves as the ministry's spokesman in the Cabinet and transmits to the ministry the policy decisions and directives of the Prime Minister and Cabinet. He is also responsible for the execution of such policy and, together with his deputy minister or ministers, undersecretaries, and the directors-general who head the departments, provides coordination of ministerial activities. The minister receives staff assistance from an Office of the Secretary to the Min-

ister, whose head is also a political appointee, presumably personally loyal to the minister. One or two deputy ministers normally
will assist the minister in both policy and administrative matters.

Immediately below the minister and directly responsible to
him is the permanent undersecretary, who is the highest ranking
career officer of the ministry. It is his responsibility to provide
general administrative supervision over the activities of the departments within the ministry. He directs an Office of the Undersecretary which, in turn, is divided into divisions and sections. This
Office of the Undersecretary contains various central administrative
services such as a Central Division (for intra-ministry communications, records, general paperwork) and a Finance Division (to
develop a ministerial budget on the basis of departmental budgetary
requirements). One or more deputy undersecretaries may provide
the undersecretary with assistance in his myriad of detailed administrative activities.

The basic line agencies of a ministry are its departments. A
ministry will normally have anywhere from four to eight departments, depending upon its size and functions. There are about sixty
departments in the government. Each department is headed by a
director-general and may also have one or more deputy directors-
general. The directors-general and deputies, although senior career
civil servants, customarily must be acceptable to the Prime Minister and often have some political influence derived from association with a previous successful coup d'etat. Directors-general
have sometimes been changed as a result of new coups, however.
Given the fact that the departments are relatively self-contained,
controlling their own budgets and being actively engaged in personnel administration, and the concurrent fact that they are the
primary operational units of the adminstrative system, the directors-
general are in a very strong position in any given regime. They
exercise direct administrative supervision and control over their
departmental subordinates.

Departments are composed of an Office of the Secretary (to
assist the director-general), Central and Technical Divisions (to

provide certain central services), and several line divisions composed of sections and headed by division chiefs. It is these divisions and their sections which employ the bulk of Thai civil servants and conduct most of the day-to-day business of Thai public administration.

In addition to the regular structure outlined above, there are also a large number of autonomous and semiautonomous agencies, including public corporations, which function at the national level of administration. Ultimately, whatever their relationship to a specific ministry, their leadership is also responsible to the Prime Minister. As noted earlier, official Thai statistics have indicated the existence of about 130 such agencies.

As indicated in earlier discussion of the integrative capabilities of the contemporary system, general territorial administration is organized in terms of seventy-one provinces and their districts, subdistricts, communes, villages, and hamlets. Functioning essentially as agencies of national administration, these geographic units are under the direct control of provincial governors and their district officers, all of whom are national civil servants and officials of the Department of Interior within the Ministry of Interior. The system roughly parallels the French prefectorial system, but lacks even the degree of local self-government characteristic of that highly centralized and unitary pattern. It is, then, preeminently a system of national territorial administration rather than of local government.

PERSONNEL ADMINISTRATION

Contemporary personnel administration within the civil service system has legal roots in a preliminary statute of 1928 under the absolute monarchy, as well as in a National Civil Service Law of 1933. These laws were designed to modernize and westernize (particularly along British lines) but not destroy the career system which had developed up to that time. As a result, the contemporary system, like the larger political system, blends the old and the new, with Western forms frequently functioning on the basis of Thai custom and traditional behavior.

A national Civil Service Commission, located within the Office of the President of the Council of Ministers and with the Prime Minister as its ex officio head, legally is responsible for government-wide regulation and supervision. In addition to the Prime Minister, it is composed of the deputy prime minister(s) and five to seven regular members. The Commission's chief functions are to maintain central personnel files, develop uniform personnel regulations, approve the establishment of new civil service positions, set entrance and promotion requirements, supervise Thai students studying abroad, evaluate academic degrees for pay purposes, review selection and disciplinary practices, and hear appeals from disciplinary actions taken within the service. It has a staff of about 170 persons.

In actual operation, the national Civil Service Commission provides general guidance and supervision rather than active leadership and control. Recruitment, selection, promotion, discipline, training, and employee welfare activities are performed primarily at the ministerial, departmental, and provincial levels. Salary schedules are determined by statutes.

The ministries and departments have civil service subcommittees, authorized by the National Civil Service Law, which are assigned major legal responsibilities for personnel administration, including the preparation and administration of entrance examinations. Within a ministry, the subcommittee is composed of the minister, undersecretary, and directors-general. Within a department, it is composed of the director-general, deputy directors-general, and division chiefs. Within a province, the governor and heads of the central government's local field units form the subcommittee. There are also a wide variety of ad hoc committees.

In practice, the senior line officers—including the undersecretaries, directors-general, deputy directors-general, and division and section chiefs—bear the primary responsibility for personnel administration. They determine the final selection of new entrants into the service, are able to assign duties, recommend promotions and pay increases, discipline and transfer their subordinate personnel. Within the framework of general national law and standards, therefore, the line agencies of the administrative system dominate personnel administration.

Civil servants are grouped into five classes based upon rank, in the European manner, rather than on function or job. These classes range downward from special through fourth class. An individual's class normally determines his position, although there is some limited definition of job functions and technical qualifications. Secondary-school graduates enter as fourth-class officials upon successful completion of examinations based largely on their education. Thereafter, a limited number are able to work their way up through four grades until, through seniority, personal acceptability to superiors, and successful completion of third-class entrance examinations, they achieve promotion to the third class. The overwhelming majority, however, remain in the fourth class but receive regular salary increases related to their grade within the class. In 1962, 82.8 percent of the Thai civil service was in this class and working at clerical or similar levels (including primary schoolteachers).

University graduates enter the system as third-class officials after passing competitive examinations which somewhat exceed the breadth and level of knowledge demanded in fourth-class entrance examinations. All officials in this class are potentially promotable to the highest positions in the public service. In 1962, 10.8 percent of the civil servants were in the third class, working mainly as nonsupervisory section officials. An academic degree beyond the baccalaureate entitles its holder to a higher salary step within the two grades which compose the third class. Upon advancing through annual salary increases to within a step or two of the highest salary levels for his class, the third-class official normally becomes eligible for promotion to the second class. Actual promotion, however, also requires recommendation by his superior, passing of a qualifying examination (which often is a formality), and approval of his ministry's civil service subcommission. There must also be a higher position available to him.

Second-class officials (4.9% of the total), first-class officials (1.1%), and special-class officials (.4%) generally follow the same promotion pattern for career advancement, although special-class status requires ministerial recommendation and approval by the Thai Cabinet. Almost all of the positions in these top classes are filled on the basis of seniority after initial entry into the service in the third class. Second-class officials are usually section chiefs and deputy district officers; first-class officials are division chiefs or district officers; and special-class officials serve as undersecretaries, directors-general, provincial governors, judges, and senior university professors.

Thus, the regular civil service provides the ambitious young Thai with an elaborate official, hierarchical structure within which he can acquire increasing amounts of social status, power and even access to wealth at the highest levels. Moreover, this opportunity has been made available to all Thai with the requisite formal education. Through the bureaucracy, access can be gained to the country's ruling class and even to its governing elite. The fact that the cultural and behavioral characteristics of the bureaucracy are rooted in traditional Thai culture links this ruling class, despite its Western overtones, to the masses of the society. The Thai civil service, therefore, provides the educated equivalent of Napoleon's drummer boy with an opportunity to achieve the administrative equivalent of a Marshal's baton, while the Thai Armed Forces provide the same opportunity in even more literal terms. By so doing, the country obtains bureaucratic leadership with some of the characteristics of a "natural" aristocracy. An important result is popular acceptance of that leadership, a major contribution to societal stability.

Administrative Modernization Requirements

The outline of the Thai administrative system provided in the preceding section obviously suggests that the country is able to perform basic governmental functions in a fashion which has proved acceptable to both the majority of the population and to the national elites. This acceptance has resulted from the administrative system's rooting in national culture, effective absorption of many educated and achievement-oriented persons, identification with the governing elite, historic acceptance of periodic though limited reform designed to introduce a measure of modernization, and previous problem-solving capabilities. Nevertheless, it also has been emphasized that the public administrative system is excessively conservative, concerned chiefly with the preservation of the national status quo, and manipulated in behalf of political cliques and bureaucratic self-interest. It is, therefore, in a transitional stage of development from the perspective of mid-twentieth century modernity and requires significant improvement if it is to continue to meet national needs. Its chief modernization requirements may be identified and summarized as follows:

(1) *Greater External and Developmental-Oriented Political Control*

The point has been made repeatedly that the Thai state is militarized and bureaucratized. As a result, its political underdevelopment is much greater than its administrative. As a product of this underdevelopment, the administrative system does not receive the necessary goal orientation, guidance, control, and supervision consonant with national developmental needs—political, social, economic, and cultural. Obviously, this is not so much an internal weakness of the bureaucracy, per se, as of the entire polity. Nevertheless, without further political modernization, it is difficult to visualize bureaucratic provision of development leadership either in its own internal transformation or in the future modernization of the country. Its fundamental conservatism and elitist-vested interests appear to impose major restrictions on such self-reform. The only real hope within the present pattern is that better and more modern education of Thai bureaucrats will lead to positive modifications in their values and behavior.

(2) *Reduced Intervention into Administrative Operations for Nonpolicy Reasons*

The point also has been made that the ruling military oligarchy engages in excessive intervention in the operation of the administrative system for reasons which have more to do with spoils than with program. This is obviously antithetical to administrative efficiency and morality. To improve Thai public administrative capabilities, such intervention must therefore be reduced. Again, one faces the question as to whether or not the regime can engage in such reform of practices which, it should be added, have been accepted with considerable complacency by most Thai because of traditional cultural attitudes.

(3) *Reduction of Behavioral Practices Antagonistic to Efficiency and Effectiveness*

There are several types of bureaucratic behavior, rooted in Thai culture and tradition, which are in conflict with program-oriented, developmental administration and which therefore require modernization. Excessive subservience and deference to superiors, for example, leads individuals to devote more attention to pleasing and cultivating their bosses than to efficient and productive job performance. The superiors, for their part, tend to demand of their subordinates that they perform personal, nonprofessional service both within and outside the job relationship as evidence of merit. Such attitudes obviously manifest the secondary concern for substantive accomplishment which characterizes most Thai civil servants. They constitute an abuse of administrative authority by superiors and also make it very difficult for subordinates to provide superiors with constructive recommendations for the improvement of operations. In the case of younger officials who have been exposed to Western education and are anxious to increase the system's modernity, their insertion into such traditional relationships can only produce frustration and even despair while depriving the government of the effective services of would-be modernizers.

Similarly, the behavioral rules for "getting ahead" in Thai society, in general, as well as within the bureaucracy, in particular, also emphasize a traditional form of gamesmanship based upon "face," and individual maneuver for power and status through personal favor or fear rather than a competition for substantive accomplishment. There also is much behind-the-scenes formation of temporary alliances designed to promote the positions of some bureaucrats and destroy those of others, again without great concern for program achievement. This atmosphere, in turn, causes superiors to avoid the risks of taking meaningful disciplinary action against subordinates for fear of unknown forms of retaliation. Punishments are mild, therefore, or transfer possibly coupled with promotion may be used to get rid of an erring or incompetent subordinate in this situation.

In addition, tradition combined with very inadequate salaries encourages misuse of official positions for personal gain. Various degrees of bribery and corruption are tolerated as normal and, even when exposed, do not usually cause major crises or great efforts "to clean house." Cooperative effort and team spirit, moreover, are not normal to Thai behavior either within or outside the bureaucracy. Loyalty to "the organization" is not customary. This, too, helps to create an atmosphere of personal career adventurism in which it is difficult for any official to rely upon the loyalty and commitment (personal or program) of his colleagues and subordinates.

(4) *Reduced Centralization of Decision-Making*

The nature of Thai politics and political leadership combines with cultural emphasis on hierarchy, respect for superiors, the desire not to lose "face," and the lack of confidence of superiors in subordinates to produce a situation in which decisions are habitually passed upwards rather than made at appropriate administrative levels. Even ministers have been known to avoid decisions appropriate to their positions and, instead, seek action by the Cabinet or the Prime Minister. Moreover, where an official is willing to assume decision-making responsibilities, he often finds that established procedures as well as the attitude of his superiors seriously restricts his discretionary authority. This contributes greatly to administrative inefficiency as well as to red tape. It also encourages lack of individual initiative for substantive program purposes. Where decisions must be made, there is a tendency to do so by committee in order to avoid the onus of individual responsibility.

(5) *Increased Numbers of Technically Trained Personnel*

Despite the traditional prestige of the public service and the still limited competition provided it by private enterprise, there is a serious shortage of technically trained personnel capable of staffing a modern administrative system. This results in part from the fact that recruitment is geared almost exclusively to the general educational system, in part from traditional Thai disinterest in technical training, and in part from still inadequate technical training facilities within the public administrative system. While steady expansion of in-service training has been occurring, severe shortages remain at almost all levels, ranging from clerical and office management skills through supervisory and managerial techniques. These shortages not only reduce efficiency but often make it necessary for senior administrators to hold several positions at once, with resultant lessening of their ability to make the maximum contribution to any one role.

(6) *Reduced Emphasis on Hierarchical Rank at the Expense of Functional Specialization*

The rank-classification system, particularly when operative within Thai culture and in conjunction with serious shortages of technically trained personnel, muddies functional differentiation among jobs. It reduces the possibility of promoting and rewarding civil servants primarily in terms of their actual substantive capabilities and contributions. The comparative measurement of efficient performance among employees by a supervisor is also extremely difficult. This situation facilitates promotion and pay increases for reasons other than performance efficiency and also increases the inclination of the supervisor to concentrate on the maintenance of stability and hierarchy rather than to promote productivity.

(7) *More Adequate Overall Coordination*

Since ministries, departments, and even divisions function substantively in semiautonomy, the administrative system suffers from a lack of effective coordination. Responsibility for specific functions is often dispersed among a number of people located in different administrative units. This leads to excessive duplication of activities and of staff in a system which is short of skilled personnel and financial resources. It also prevents maximum impact from being made in the performance of a given function and contributes to bureaucratic jurisdictional rivalries. In addition, effective use of personnel is limited by the fact that movement among departments and ministries is very limited. Civil servants normally make their careers within the confines of a single agency, regardless of needs or opportunities in other sectors of the administrative system.

(8) *More Use of Modern-Management Staff Aids*

Research consciousness has not developed to any great extent among Thai administrators. In addition, trained researchers are sufficiently in short supply so that the assistance available from this source is extremely limited, in any event. Moreover, the superior-subordinate relationship generated within Thai culture makes the former reluctant to seek the advice of the latter. Superiors are supposed to be more knowledgeable and more virtuous, and their traditional role is to provide direction to subordinates rather than to consult with them. As a result, a relative handful of top administrators, personally overextended because of their need to fill several jobs concurrently, do not have adequate staff assistance available to them and, moreover, are culturally reluctant to use what they have. Their assistants are equally reluctant to do more than carry out specific orders.

(9) *More Adequate Placement Policy*

Because rank rather than job classification is employed in the personnel system, meaningful job descriptions are rare, recruitment into the service is in terms of formal nontechnical education, and in-service training is still limited. As a result, civil servants are not placed to make the greatest substantive contributions. Individual qualifications and skills are not effectively matched with job requirements. Agencies make personnel requests primarily in terms of academic degree and rank, not training and related experience. Thailand's available human resources, therefore, are not utilized with maximum efficiency from the point of view of substantive, programmatic accomplishment.

(10) *More Adequate Management Services*

There are a variety of key modern-management services which are underdeveloped in the Thai administrative system. Thai statistical services, for example, are not yet on a sound operational basis although efforts at improvement have been occurring for a number of years. In part, this weakness has stemmed from inadequate official appreciation of the need for collecting, collating, and analyzing meaningful statistics. The general lack of preoccupation with program accomplishment would, in large measure, explain this attitude. In addition, there is probably a certain hesitancy to detail too greatly some of the activities and conditions which prevail since this may focus attention on abuses and misuses of official positions. Indicative of the problem is the observation of the International Bank for Reconstruction and Development (sometimes referred to as the World Bank) report of 1958 that the Central Statistical Office, which is the principal agency in this area, had at that time no trained statistician on its staff of more than 50, while few if any of the ministerial and departmental statistical units had personnel with more than the most elementary in-service training, despite the designation of 370 people as "statis-ticians." [3] Even after a number of American and United Nations technical assistance programs in this field, any sophisticated statis-tical analysis such as the 1960 census still required foreign pro-fessional leadership.

Financial administration is another area in which considerable improvement remains necessary.[4] The budget process has deficien-cies which range from forms and techniques, through accounting and reporting procedures, to excessively inflated and relatively unsubstantiated appropriations requests from the departments and ministries to the Ministry of Finance. The latter, for its part, has been inadequately organized and staffed in the past to engage in modern budget preparation.

In addition, fiscal auditing and control techniques have been extremely inadequate. Expenditures sometimes exceed budgeted appropriations in a given year, important sources of public funds such as the National Lottery normally have not been included in the central auditing and budgeting system, and many of the public enterprises are supervised in uneven and irregular fashion.

As a result of such inadequacies in financial administration, it was estimated by some highly informed observers that, at least prior to 1958, as much as 20 percent of government income was misappropriated to the personal advantage of possibly 400 mem-bers of the ruling oligarchy. In 1964, after the death of Marshal Sarit, the Thai press carried feature stories reportedly based on findings of government investigators which indicated that as much as $18 million in public funds was intermingled with the Marshal's estate, which reputedly was at least $140 million. Marshal Sarit had long controlled the National Lottery, as well as participating as a director in innumerable public, semipublic, and private enter-prises. The published accounts of his finances, after his death, were reminiscent of similar accounts provided by Marshal Sarit's

[3] *Ibid.*, pp. 216–217.
[4] *Ibid.*, pp. 198–207.

government about the corruption of his predecessors when he overthrew Marshal Phibun and Police General Phao in 1957.

No meaningful management analysis is undertaken within the Thai system, another area of weakness. There is no network of organization and methods units at the various administrative levels to scrutinize operations and develop proposals for administrative reform and improvement. Since 1963, there has been an Administrative Organization and Regulation Advisory Board responsible for developing reorganization plans. However, to date, no comprehensive reorganization program has been announced. Obstacles to this type of scrutiny are cultural—based upon suspicion of motives and hesitancy about the use of all forms of staff aid—as well as practical—based upon the lack of skilled personnel and the administrative desire not to be scrutinized too closely.

Planning, too, is an area of weakness although Thailand finally introduced a development plan for 1961–1966, based largely upon the 1958 recommendations of the World Bank report and formulated under a National Economic Development Board. It has since announced a second such plan for 1967–1971. Nevertheless, the planning mechanisms are not yet fully developed, and certain of the important administrative recommendations of the World Bank have not been completely implemented. Planning personnel, too, like statistical personnel, are in serious short supply. Moreover, the Thai approach is primarily an economic approach, and does not consider the extent to which economic growth is dependent on political, administrative, social, and cultural change.

In sum, to quote from Professor Fred W. Riggs, "From one point of view, the structure of the government seems to be a model of organizational symmetry and structural simplicity." On this basis, one could conclude that it is far more rational than the American system. But, as Riggs also notes, the "essential question is not the formal or intrinsic rationality of the organizational design, but rather the motivational forces which give it life." [5] In the Thai case, the motivations are not yet sufficiently modern and

[5] Riggs, p. 347.

the underlying operation of the administrative machinery is not yet sufficiently efficient or effective to provide the country with a strong administrative capability for societal development. The system works, but not primarily for the purposes which are now becoming determinants of future national survival.

CHAPTER VI

🌀

The Thai Government
and Development:
A Strategic Evaluation

Development Potential: A Balance Sheet

Previous discussion has suggested both the basic assets and the major inadequacies of Thailand as it struggles to survive and prosper in the contemporary world. They might be summarized briefly in a balance sheet for development as follows:

ASSETS FOR DEVELOPMENT

1. *Natural Resources.* The country is blessed by large blocks of alluvial soil, substantial rainfall, and a considerable number of rivers and streams which have been supplemented by canals. These natural assets have made it one of the richest rice-producing areas in the world and have provided most of the population with assured and easily attained subsistence. Important supplementation of this natural economic foundation is provided by fruit, forest products, and fish—all of which can also be obtained by most of the population without great effort. Extensive rubber cultivation and tin

mining has proved possible, moreover, even with the use of very simple methods. All of these resources, plus a limited number of additional ones, are capable of further development.

2. *Demography*. Within this reasonably well-provided land reside a people who are still sufficiently few in number to avoid that overpopulation and pressure upon natural resources from which most Asians suffer. Moreover, because of their historic commitment to agriculture, they are not excessively concentrated and harassed by urban problems.

3. *Education*. A substantial educational system already exists which provides the masses with literacy, offers people of varying social status some opportunity for advanced education, and constitutes a primary basis for entry into the governing elite.

4. *Culture and Behavior*. A majority of the population is effectively integrated into a common culture whose development through centuries within an independent country has given them a sense of national identity. It is a culture, moreover, which, while providing social-psychological cohesion, has manifested sufficient flexibility to permit various past modifications of traditionalism by national leadership in the interest of limited modernization. It is also a culture which does not easily spawn revolution, provides ethical possibilities for improvement in one's condition, and emphasizes a respect for authority which contributes to national stability. In combination with the population's ability to feed and sustain itself with relatively little effort, and the absence of widespread feelings of oppression, it has produced a reasonably complacent and happy people.

5. *Social Structures*. Rural society, which encompasses approximately 85 percent of the population, is relatively undisturbed by socio-economic tensions. Relationships are essentially traditional, generally acceptable to all, and devoid of feelings of class oppression. Within the small urban society, relationships among various status groups, although much more elaborately structured than in rural society, also do not reveal tensions presently capable of destroying national unity or of producing revolution. Access

151

to the governing elite is not restricted by heredity or caste or even wealth, and historic accommodations continue to prevail.

6. *Economy.* As already suggested, the country's primary natural resources have made possible a strong agricultural economic foundation which has been further enhanced by rubber cultivation and the mining of rich tin reserves. With only limited population pressure, and a favorable international market for surpluses of basic Thai products, this economic foundation has provided a reasonably good standard of living in Asian terms. The country is not wracked by destitution and starvation, viewed from its own or an Asian perspective. It also offers opportunities for further economic growth in various sectors.

7. *Government.* Despite its traditionalism, conservatism, and lack of popularization, the Thai government is well rooted in the national political culture. It is also heir to centuries of experience in self-government, is based upon a pool of bureaucrats who have had advanced education, has not been oppressive as far as the masses of Thai are concerned, and is accepted with complacency by most of the populace. Its capabilities are such that it has been able to perform at least the basic functions of government sufficiently well to maintain a high measure of political stability and to preserve national security and independence.

OBSTACLES AND INADEQUACIES FOR DEVELOPMENT

1. *Location.* The Thai location in the center of the Southeast Asian peninsula is basically a liability in the contemporary era. Its historic accessibility remains at a time when aggressive Chinese and North Vietnamese Communism is at its borders, with few natural barriers of consequence to help protect the kingdom. The chief saving feature is that the Thai location on the China Sea does permit the country's major ally—the United States—to reach it and to provide defensive assistance through control of the sea and air lanes. Nevertheless, for reasons of international politics, the Thai location places the country in great jeopardy and makes it possible for Communist agents to infiltrate from several neighboring coun-

tries, attempt to stimulate rebellion, and otherwise to promote chaos.

2. *Natural Resources.* Although much rich alluvial soil exists, the Northeast, with one-third of the total land area, contains poor soil and receives a very inadequate supply of water. Moreover, throughout the nation there is a serious shortage of important mineral deposits. The known Thai natural resource base, therefore, is limited chiefly to the cultivable soil, forests, fish supply, and tin.

3. *Health, Sanitation, Housing, and Diet.* Although the Thai condition in this regard generally is good by Asian standards, it is far below that of countries like Japan and is in need of considerable improvement as part of modernization. When combined with a generally debilitating climate, these inadequacies are bound to affect the vigor of the population and its productive capabilities.

4. *Education and Training.* Despite the substantial educational base developed to date, Thailand is still at the bottom of a list of the semiadvanced nations of the world. Its major inadequacies are not so much quantitative as qualitative, not only in terms of general education but even more particularly in terms of scientific, technological, and managerial training capable of providing critical modern skills.

5. *Manpower Resources.* The labor force remains overwhelmingly an agricultural one which lacks significant modern cultivation skills. The small nonagricultural work force, moreover, also is characterized by its serious shortage of almost all forms of modern skills.

6. *Culture and Behavior.* Although the Thai culture provides cohesion for a majority of the population and also has manifested some capacity for adjustment to change, such cohesion does not extend to large minority groups and receptivity to change has been limited in various ways. In the case of the latter, change has been most accepted when it has been associated with agriculture and other traditional forms of activity; it has been least accepted when related to more modern nonagricultural activities. Even then, it has had to be actively promoted by authoritative leadership, its

utility demonstrated clearly in Thai value terms, and selectivity employed in its innovation. Thus, although some modernizing changes have proved possible, there is no evidence of the ability to engage in massive transformations of the type achieved by Japan.

7. *Social Structures.* Important ethnic minorities have not yet been effectively incorporated into Thai society and are open to at least some Communist infiltration. In addition, there is a serious absence of a nonbureaucratic Thai middle class capable of providing leadership in the private economic sector and of modernizing the polity by reducing its militarism and authoritarianism.

8. *Economy.* Despite the great rice production, forest products, and tin and rubber resources, the Thai economy confronts some increasingly serious problems which must be resolved. In essence, these involve the increasing population pressure, limited growth in rice productivity to meet this pressure, and dependence of the economy for most of its economic fat above the subsistence level on the export of a few agricultural and primary products. At the same time, government requires a significant expansion of its revenue to meet security and development costs.

9. *Government.* Two major and interrelated sets of problems exist. On the political level, there is a need for greater popularization and expansion of integrative capabilities. On the administrative level, there is a serious question as to whether the present bureaucratized system is capable of developing and maintaining the necessary commitment to modernization and of implementing that commitment.

All previous discussion, as well as the preceding balance sheet, suggests that the Thai future is uncertain. Much—both national security and national well-being—depends upon the extent to which the government is seriously attempting to resolve its developmental problems. What, then, has it been doing? What guidelines are being followed in policy, strategy, and planning for development and what hope for success do they offer?

Thai Development Policy and Strategy

Major transformations of Thailand throughout its long history as a statist society have always depended upon government identification of the need for change, willingness to lead the way, and skill in achieving the established objectives. Not surprisingly in view of the traditional culture and related absence of popular revolutions, the overall perspective brought to bear by Thai rulers has been a conservative although often an enlightened one. Governmental, administrative, legal, and socio-economic reforms have been introduced which were sufficient to permit national adaptation to major pressures (more often external than internal), but which also have minimized negative impact upon the traditional sources of stability. The costs to traditional society, in other words, were kept to a minimum by avoiding revolutionary transformations which could not be controlled by government. Steeped in this historic and successful policy of carefully managed change, the present rulers of Thailand continue to apply it to the country's contemporary problems. Government policy, therefore, remains a conservative and a tutelary one designed to preserve as much of traditional society and culture as possible while promoting those improvements without which national survival might be in jeopardy.

In their application of this broad and historic policy perspective, the contemporary rulers have gradually identified the types of need for reform for whose attainment they are willing to some extent to commit themselves. By so doing, they have again demonstrated a measure of that sensitivity among Thai rulers which has enabled the country to survive in independence for so long; like many of its predecessors, the present-day leadership is not reactionary. Collectively, if not always individually, the ruling elite does recognize some of the national need for progress. Moreover, and most importantly, there is an awareness that the benefits of such progress must accrue to the Thai masses at least in terms of improved living conditions. Authoritarianism remains benevolent.

Despite the positiveness of this general identification of the need for improvement, however, two major types of question must be raised: (1) Does the present leadership comprehend the full scope of Thailand's developmental needs? (2) Does it have the skill required to achieve the necessary improvements while maintaining a stability whose traditional foundations must inevitably be modified? Is the Thai government really capable, in other words, of presiding successfully over a new stage of national development in which there will be further modernization without chaos and revolution? To the extent that the answers to these questions may not be strongly affirmative, Thailand will increasingly be in trouble and communism's opportunities will be enhanced.

Political Development

As one surveys the activities of the Thai leadership since 1932 (and particularly since the 1950's), it becomes clear that the identification of developmental needs has been limited and fragmented, although realistic as far as it has gone. As a result, operative policy, strategy, plans, and programs have reflected the same characteristics. Understandably, the major inadequacy in the definition of developmental needs and objectives has been political. Given the self-selecting and often self-serving character of the ruling circles— and the political culture and heritage in which they are well rooted —they have not demonstrated a willingness to engage in any major reformation of the regime. In fact, they have not even been willing to institutionalize and regularize authoritarianism, let alone move toward a popularization of government. Instead, this militarized oligarchy which, for the past ten years, has had an even less representative base than between 1932 and 1958 and is only now about to reestablish the limited popular participation of the past in a new constitution, draws heavily upon its historic and traditional assets, as if the pool will never run dry and popular political behavior will never change. In this one respect, it does border on the reactionary. It seems to assume the indefinite perpetuation of mass political apathy, cultural respect for hierarchy and authority, and the unifying and symbolic value of the monarchy. It generally seems to take the position that the political forces of modernity (both democratic and totalitarian) will not affect the Thai people as long as the national borders are preserved, some significant economic growth is registered, various public welfare services are improved upon, and the regime does not tyrannize its citizenry. It proclaims that the Thai people are not ready for Western political democracy (which may very well be true), that Thai political culture and traditions call for something other than Western political democracy (certainly true up to the present), and that the serious Communist threat to the country does not permit experimentation which may produce political instability and perhaps chaos.

With the preceding political beliefs and fears as its justification for keeping the status quo—and possibly also because it does not know how to modify the regime without losing control—the current leadership continues to rule by improvisation. As discussed earlier, it has no regular means for succession to power other than by military coup d'etat; and no effort has been made to modernize the regime by expanding its political base beyond the estimated 2 percent of the population which now constitutes the political public and from which derives the ruling elite. It is assumed that the new generations of achievement-oriented Thai, like their parents, will find their places within the established order and not contest it from outside. The leadership appears to ignore the political potential in that expansion and modernization of education and in that gradual growth of the new Thai private entrepreneurial class which it is fostering, just as it seems not to realize that the infiltration of modern political ideas among the urbanized elites also is increasing rapidly and, some day, will seep down to the masses as well.

Since the 1958 coup, therefore, the regime has been asserting that it is working on a new constitution. That this was not being done with enthusiasm was demonstrated on several occasions. During July 1965, for example, the appointed Constituent Assembly assigned the task became involved in debate over proposed amendments to a draft constitution submitted to it by the government six months earlier. In the ensuing discussion, both the Premier (Marshal Thanom) and the next most powerful man of the kingdom, General Prapat (Deputy Premier, Interior Minister, and Army Commander-in-Chief) publicly reasserted their conviction that the Thai people were not prepared for democracy and that a new constitution must be rooted in the principles of Marshal Sarit's 1958 coup d'etat. That coup, as previously mentioned, had banned political parties, elections, and trade unions, and otherwise had tightened authoritarian controls over the society.

Thus, the present regime has, during the last ten years, avoided responsibility for producing any constructive alternatives. Popularization of government may have to be limited and "guided" in accordance with Thai requirements, but the country certainly needs something more than self-seeking improvisation based upon military coups and rooted in traditionalism. It should at least catch up to the Bismarckian level of political development operating in Imperial Germany prior to 1918. Even in less-developed, half-Communist Laos and in devastated South Vietnam, as well as in Malaysia, Singapore, and the Philippines, some form of electoral system and some gestures toward popular participation in national politics are being made. Long-term stability and the preservation of national independence depend upon acts of political creativity now, in advance of turmoil. Thailand does not have to ape the Western democracies, but it cannot continue to ignore indefinitely the twentieth-century goal of some form of mass participation in the political process. This is not an age in which government can count on popular political apathy and submissiveness as a permanent feature of any society.

After all, there are two groups of regular Communist cadres in Thailand, organized into two parties: the Communist Party of Thailand (with 200–300 members in 1963) and the Chinese Communist Party in Thailand (with 3,000–4,000 members and supporters in 1963). Their members have been primarily intellectuals and workers, and their organizations date back to 1935 for the Thai and about 1925 for the Chinese.[1] Though still small in numbers up to the present, their potential has now been considerably enhanced by the existence on the Thai-Malaysia border of the 500-man hard-core remnant of the Communist Party of Malaya (which operates and proselytizes on both sides), by the success of the Pathet Lao (which controls at least half of that neighboring country), and by the new Peking- and Hanoi-sponsored revolutionary warfare campaigns against Thailand. In regard to the latter, some 1967 estimates suggest that there are from 1,000 to 5,000 active guerrillas (with base camps) and possibly as many as 50,000 or more potential peasant sympathizers in the Northeast, plus other Communist agents among the 35,000 Vietnamese resident in Thailand and evidences of some guerrillas both on the Burmese and Cambodian borders.[2] Since revolutionary warfare is political as well as military warfare, the Thai government cannot limit its response primarily to an expansion of its police forces.

While a foreign observer cannot, at long distance, prescribe the specifics of the required political innovation, it would certainly seem that the polity's participatory capabilities should, at a minimum, be expanded to the extent of again having one-half of the legislature popularly elected, as called for under the new draft constitution. Although this arrangement, with its appointive Senate, clearly protects the government from excessive popular political pressure, the important thing is that some electoral opportunity be provided the general public so that it gains experience in political self-government. Similarly, self-government at the village, provincial, and municipal levels should be expanded. This is important not just for the political experience it will provide, but also as a means of further committing the masses to the polity and thereby promoting both politicization and integration. Measures

[1] Based on Robert A. Scalapino, ed., *The Communist Revolution in Asia* (Englewood Cliffs, N.J.: Prentice-Hall, 1965), pp. 10, 13, 32–33 and 229–230.

[2] By-line dispatches from the Thai Northeast by Peter Arnett, Associated Press, July 15, 1967 and Kim Willenson, United Press International, July 19, 1967 and July 21, 1967.

of this sort are particularly critical in the Thai-Lao Northeast and the Thai-Malay South, current requirements probably exceeding the initial gestures of the government in those regions. Viable government in the present age, since it requires popular support and not just acquiescence, cannot be produced solely by bureaucratic action; it requires some form of political participation by the masses as well as the elites.

Finally, major efforts to increase the honesty of government must be made; a proper relationship between political leadership and the bureaucracy established; and, eventually, civil leadership must replace the military, with succession to power a product of institutionalized selection procedures rather than military coup. The Thai political tradition is, indeed, one of strong executive leadership, and it may well be that this characteristic should be continued indefinitely for cultural and practical reasons. Nevertheless, it should not be forgotten that the political tradition, as it emerged by the twentieth century, also called for the rulers to behave righteously, reflect that moral virtue with which they presumably were endowed, and otherwise justify their dominance by effective performance of the political functions required in a given era. The political heritage does not provide justification for corruption and incompetence. Moreover, one must also keep in mind the fact that the so-called revolution of 1932 was conducted in the name of constitutionalism and political liberty—that it was a commitment of the new elites to political modernization. After thirty-five years of groping, Thailand must now move into a fourth phase of political development in its modern history (the Chakri kings Mongkut [Rama IV] and Chulalongkorn [Rama V] providing the first, Ramas VI and VII a second, and the 1932 destruction of royal absolutism the third). The ideological substance of 1932 must be brought to some measure of fruition.

At the administrative level, as previously noted, government already is more developed than it is politically. Some Thai intellectuals and foreign scholars argue, in fact, that as a result of this particular imbalance, the current system's effectiveness (in terms of society's needs) is actually lower than it was under the absolute monarchy, when better external political direction and control were provided. Previous discussion has identified the capability limitations which do prevail and the modernization requirements still to be achieved. American and international technical assistance have been making some positive contributions to this end with the cooperation of the Thai government, it is true. Although the regime has been careful to limit the impact of administrative reforms, an increase in administrative capabilities has been occurring, at least in a technical sense. However, it is to be hoped that such improvements, in combination with expanded emphasis on public administration education and various training programs, also will help to modernize behavioral practices. Moreover, the leadership must keep in mind the fact that administrative modernization must be associated with political modernization if maximum progress, stability, and security are to be obtained. The lesson of 1932 in this connection is clear: Without compatible political and administrative development, some new, modernized bureaucratic elite may emerge in the future, as it did then, which may also conclude that its satisfaction can only be achieved by seizure of political power.

Nation-Building

Although Thai development policy and strategy appears to be almost devoid of creative concern for political modernization, the external and internal Communist threat has been forcing the government to take some steps in the area of nation-building. It has been compelled to face the fact that the Thai-Lao and Thai-Malay, in particular, are not really effectively integrated into the society. In the past, as noted earlier, both of these large minority groups tended to be ignored. It was assumed, much in the manner of the official approach to the need for popularization of government, that established relationships and behavior patterns would prevail indefinitely. However, with most of the country's neighbors increasingly involved in Communist revolutionary warfare campaigns, with the Bangkok regime itself publicly targeted for overthrow by the Chinese and North Vietnamese Communists, and with mounting Communist infiltration of Thai minorities, the government has been compelled to launch some positive program responses.

In the case of the Thai-Lao, among whom the Communist threat is greatest at the moment, a series of information and socio-economic programs has been started in conjunction with increased police and security efforts. Thus, with major American assistance (it is estimated that as much as 90 percent of American economic aid to Thailand is now being devoted in one way or another to the problem), an Accelerated Rural Development Project was instituted in 1964 to improve the relationship between the rural population and Bangkok, to increase rural income, and to strengthen local self-government, with concentration in the six Northeast provinces. Roads have been constructed to link the villages with main highways leading to the Central Plain area for economic, communications, and security reasons. Public health, welfare, and educational efforts have been greatly expanded. Agricultural extension activities to get the farmers to shift from subsistence rice cultivation to the raising of other products more suited to regional soil and water conditions have begun. To bring these activities down to a self-help level, the provincial governors have been given greater coordinative and executive authority as well as additional staff, equipment, and funds for such regional rural development efforts. Mobile Development Units have also been established to meet immediate village needs through quick impact programs in the fields of health, education, public works, and in other forms of community development. In addition, there are now Mobile Information Teams and new radio stations which provide entertainment and popular political education, emphasizing the virtues of independent Thailand and the nature of the Communist threat. Buddhist monks have been brought into these programs, too, helping to distribute medicine and clothes to needy villagers and thereby also demonstrating their commitment to the Thai state, in which they have an official religious position.

In these and related ways, the Thai government is attempting to reform its traditional relationship with the Northeast in order to better bind the region to the country. On the other hand, professional foreign observers have noted some inadequacies in these government programs and their need for further improvement before they can be really successful in social-psychological as well as in economic growth terms. It has been observed, for example, that the success of initial programs prior to 1964 had been limited both because of fragmented administrative planning and execution and, more importantly and still pertinent, because "Thai officials in the capital and in the provinces had little understanding of the relationships between public functionaries and local populations which are necessary to secure the confidence and collaboration of the people." [3] It has also been suggested that there has been excessively high priority placed upon road building and not enough on the farmer's health, education, water supply, and agricultural income. Other important questions pertain to the need for improved local participation in programming through major expansion of local self-government and to related changes in the authoritarian attitudes of the central bureaucracy.

Up to the present, less effort has been devoted to increasing Thai-Malay integration into the national community than has been devoted to the Thai-Lao. Nevertheless, in the case of the former, too, the matter of Communist infiltration and separatism are beginning to be of some concern to Bangkok, and remedial programs are slowly being introduced. Some encouragement of village self-government is occurring, education in Malay is being permitted, secondary schools are being opened more to Thai-Malay students, and public gestures toward Islam are being engaged in by the government. Government and administration of the southern provinces in which the Thai-Malay are concentrated, however, remains largely a monopoly of ethnic Thai; and administrative attitudes require reform.

[3] Alvin Roseman, "Thailand, Laos and Cambodia: A Decade of AID," *Current History,* Vol. XLIX, No. 291 (November 1965), 274.

As to the other minorities, the various hill peoples increasingly have been viewed by Bangkok as a possible security problem. The response has been chiefly one of expanded border-control efforts. In other respects, however, they generally are still regarded as primitives, and little effort to incorporate them into the nation has been made. As for the highly important Chinese, the twentieth-century Thai approach of legal and administrative control and supervision, in combination with behind-the-scenes politico-economic accommodations, remain the predominant characteristics of the relationship. Little creative effort to promote better integration other than the official insistence upon Thai-language teaching in Chinese schools has been introduced. Fortunately, there is some evidence that the Chinese youth is increasingly willing to integrate itself into Thai society. Offsetting this, however, are other reports of Chinese Communist infiltration into the Thai-Chinese community, particularly among urban workers.

In sum, although mounting concern for national security in the face of Communist revolutionary warfare throughout Southeast Asia is producing a new Thai interest in minorities, there is as yet no really comprehensive program to integrate them more effectively into the society in accordance with their different needs and characteristics. Some important beginnings have been made, particularly among the Thai-Lao, but much remains to be done.

Cultural and Behavioral Modernization

Thai society's need for cultural and behavioral modernization as another key prerequisite to contemporary development also does not appear to be identified, as such, and assigned a priority in government policy and strategy. There does not seem to be any conscious recognition of the fact that, to some extent, a new Thai man must emerge in behavioral terms before substantial development occurs. The existing regime, through its expansion and increasing modernization of the educational and vocational training systems is, of course, helping to promote important changes in values. Nevertheless, this does not appear to be a conscious effort as part of a comprehensive national development strategy. Education remains deeply rooted in traditional patterns, and official concern is more with the increase in educational opportunities of established types than with any educational revolution specifically designed to transform and modernize behavior. Despite this apparent lack of full appreciation of the need for cultural and behavioral modernization, however, the very facts that the Ministry of Education is receiving the second largest share of government expenditures by function (approximately 17%), that new manpower skills are being transmitted, that the Thai physical condition is improving, and that a new Thai middle class is slowly emerging are bound to modify the traditional value system. It is essential, therefore, that the government recognize that its people are undergoing such changes so that it can consciously facilitate some cultural transformations essential to national development while simultaneously identifying and seeking to preserve those traditional values which it feels should be retained as worthwhile components of the Thai heritage and civilization. To ignore both the need and the actual forces at work—to let nature take its course—is to default in advance on the sophisticated and successful management of social change and national development.

In similar fashion, Thai development policy and strategy do not appear consciously to be concerned with the development of any pioneer group of modernizers. Yet the best analysis, past or present, of the process of development clearly documents the extent to which such social change occurs only when there is a creative, innovative pioneering component within a populace which is willing to spearhead the drive to break through traditionalism. In large measure, this is due to the fact that the ruling and bureaucratized elite regards itself as the only appropriate leadership group. Given the country's culture and heritage, the performance of a modernizing role by the elite could greatly facilitate national development. It has the necessary authority and position in society, and it sustains itself through absorption of new generations of educated youth. Moreover, there are no alternative private groups, at present, other than the Communist cadres. Unfortunately, however, as previously discussed, this elite has been basically conservative and more preoccupied with the preservation of stability than with creative innovation. Its stimulation since 1958 of nonagricultural private enterprise among ethnic Thai, for example, undoubtedly has not been performed with the desire to create a new and competitive elite external to the bureaucracy. Moreover, the lack of strict conflict-of-interest regulations has meant that senior government officials often have taken positions as directors on the governing boards of these enterprises, thereby linking them to some extent to the public sector which these officials dominate. It should also be recalled that trade unions and political parties have been prohibited, thus restricting their leadership potential.

Where conscious efforts have been made to create new economic roles, therefore, they have been designed either to encourage Thai to replace Chinese middlemen, businessmen, and white collar workers for reasons of security and ethnic nationalism; to help modernize Thai manpower; or even to promote economic diversification. However, the motivation has not been one of creating socio-economic pioneers who will help to restructure Thai society. It seems accurate to say, therefore, that government promotion of private innovative and entrepreneurial groups capable of leading a modernization revolution has been more inadvertent than planned. Some governmental programs to modernize manpower and the economy may very well eventually lead to the emergence of such groups, but this essential step in the development process is not really a part of conscious national design. The national leadership does not appear to be interested in major behavioral or structural reform even when it is committed to an improvement of mass welfare and an increase of standards of living through controlled economic growth.

Economic Development

Apart from a priority emphasis on the expansion of public health and education, a gradual modernization of the public administrative system, and a new security-conscious concern for the regional development and politicization of the Thai-Lao Northeast, Thai developmental efforts since World War II have been chiefly fiscal and economic. Acting with caution and moderation—but, nevertheless, *acting*—the several governments steadily have been recording some significant progress which offers solid hope for the national future, provided that comparable and compatible results can be obtained in time in the political, social, and cultural spheres of life.

Between 1850 and 1950, such economic growth as did occur was largely unplanned and relatively unaided, involving chiefly a natural expansion of rice production, tin mining, and teakwood cutting in response to a growing export market. During that first century of gradual emergence from a completely traditional economy, the government avoided any serious industrialization efforts. Whatever actions were taken were chiefly administrative, legal, and fiscal; and they were intended at most to bolster the security of the subsistence farmer, facilitate the participation of specialized commercial agriculture in international trade, generally control rapacious exploitation of the land, somewhat improve public transportation and communications systems, introduce some regulations to protect Thai farmers from exploitive mill owners (most of whom were and are Chinese), maintain law and order in the countryside, and conceal the impact of taxes by imposing them indirectly. In the very small commercial and manufacturing sectors which began to emerge at the beginning of the twentieth century, the government pursued the twin policy objectives of lessening Chinese economic domination and enlarging Thai participation in nonagricultural activity. It did so by promoting Thai entry into certain trades, white collar positions, and skilled worker jobs while simultaneously imposing legal restrictions on the Chinese practice of these occupations. It also introduced some protective labor legislation in behalf of the tiny industrial work force and some very limited social insurance and welfare programs.

By limiting its role in the economy to the types of activity just given, the Thai government successfully perpetuated the agricultural character of the society; avoided the emergence of a large, propertyless, and potentially revolutionary urban proletariat; and satisfied the basic needs of its rural masses, 85 to 89 percent of whom continued to own their land. The polity remained stable, the other key structural-functional systems well-integrated with and subordinate to it, and the country was guided slowly through the initial stage of a transitional era with the minimum of internal disruption or tension.

With the conclusion of World War II, however, during which Thailand officially had been a Japanese ally and had been rewarded by territory in neighboring lands at the expense of the British and French empires, several major new economic problems occurred. Some war reparations had to be paid Britain in the form of rice and restoration of lands; serious inflationary pressures had to be dealt with; and, after the Korean War boom, Thai exports were hard hit by a world trade recession. The customary soundness of its currency was weakened and its usual trade surplus became a substantial trade deficit. These conditions compelled the government to engage in major financial reforms designed to increase national revenue, to revise the method of financing new deficits, and to regulate exports and otherwise control currency exchange transactions.

While experimenting in this regard, however, it also became increasingly apparent that the additional growth needed for national economic well-being required more active and broader governmental leadership than had been provided in the past. Sizeable investments had to be made in the economy, and structural reforms had to be planned and promoted. Since Thai public and private financial resources were extremely limited and modern economic skills of all types were in short supply, the Thai government was compelled to turn abroad for assistance. Quite naturally, it looked primarily to both the International Bank for Reconstruction and Development and to the United States, whose sympathy had led to the limiting of British war claims against Thailand and whose desire to frustrate Communist expansionism had involved it in major schemes to help friendly countries promote their national security and economic development.

From 1949 on, therefore, Thailand negotiated a series of loans with the World Bank to finance improved irrigation in the Chao Phraya Basin, expand and modernize the Port of Bangkok, modernize the national railway system, and launch the large Yanhee hydroelectric power and irrigation complex. In addition, in 1950, the government also signed an initial Economic and Technical Cooperation Agreement with the United States, which provided the basis for its becoming a recipient of American foreign aid. During the period of 1951–1954, the resultant American economic aid averaged about $6 million annually, with the amount increasing to an average of almost $30 million annually from 1955 on. With these American grants and loans, and the accompanying technical assistance, Thailand was helped and encouraged to engage in a large variety of new programs designed to modernize and develop its human resources, expand various government public welfare services, increase its investment in social overhead capital development, introduce agricultural diversification, and modernize various aspects of the public administrative system. Simultaneously, the United States provided a large degree of help in the enlargement and improvement of conventional Thai police and armed forces in order to increase national security. More limited degrees of special assistance also were obtained by the government from the United Nations and a number of foreign countries other than the United States.

Through these various forms of foreign and international assistance the government steadily improved its and the country's general economic condition. The currency was put back on a sound basis, and some important steps were taken to modify the economy and increase its basic soundness by improving its substructure. Some limited and not too successful efforts were also made to expand industrialization by the establishment of a variety of relatively small government enterprises, the creation of a National Economic Development Corporation (1954), and the provision of various guarantees and benefits to private enterprise under an Industrial Promotion Act of 1954. Nevertheless, no economic revolutions were sought or achieved and, in fact, Thailand became increasingly conspicuous for its lack of a national economic development plan in an age in which almost all countries had turned to such blueprints if for no other purpose than publicly to demonstrate their commitment to development. Economic progress was being pursued prior to 1961 (the opening year of the first economic development plan), therefore, without comprehensive planning or meaningful planning mechanisms, and on the basis of pragmatic and fragmented efforts which were subject to conflicting and self-interested political pressures among the cliques of the Thai ruling elite.

As a result of the economic and social policies being applied, whose guidelines were attitudinal more than analytical and were rooted in the policies of Thai governments between 1850 and 1945, traditional characteristics were modified but not drastically changed. The economy remained basically agricultural, with some 85 percent of the population still engaged in cultivation, forestry, and fishing. Rice continued to be the principal product, with possibly 70 percent of the total population being engaged in raising it and an officially estimated 63.1 percent of all farm land devoted to it. Nevertheless, crop and export diversification efforts also began to reduce the predominance of rice and thereby modify the economy. Thus, for example, rice's share of the total agricultural product dropped from 81 percent to 62 percent between 1950 and 1960 as its annual growth rate stayed at 1 to 2 percent while that of other products rose by far greater percentages.[4] At the same time, however, rice production was still sufficient to meet domestic consumption requirements and provide an annual surplus for export of about one million tons. It therefore remained—as it had been for a century—the country's leading export, generating almost 40 percent of all foreign exchange while the export duties imposed upon it still constituted the major source of governmental revenue.

Although rice cultivation continued to be a major economic characteristic, however, there was a significant expansion in the production of other crops, whose output between 1950 and 1960 rose approximately 18 percent. Corn, for example, now occupies the second greatest number of acres (although still just 6.1 percent of the total) and has become the fourth most valuable export although it was grown very little prior to 1950. Rubber, moreover, although just 5.3 percent of planted acreage and a crop which was introduced only after World War I, has become the second most valuable export after rice: It now produces about 22 percent of the total export income. Rubber production, in particular, has been given important aid by the government, which has been actively encouraging its development by providing technical assistance to growers and special exemptions from taxes, export duties, and licenses.

Still other evidences of this new agricultural diversification which began to occur after 1949 are provided by the expanding importance of jute and kenaf, the fact that the country has almost become self-sufficient in sugar, the development under government monopoly of a significant tobacco industry, the raising of livestock for export, and the introduction of a wide range of other farm products which are entering export channels or the urban market economy as cash crops.

[4] For a discussion of Thai agricultural modernization efforts, see U.S. Department of Agriculture, Economic Research Service, Regional Analysis Division, *Agricultural Diversification and Economic Development in Thailand: A Case Study* (Washington, D.C.: Foreign Agricultural Economic Report No. 8, March 1963).

Thailand, now the leading Asian exporter of agricultural foodstuffs, thus has made definite progress since World War II in the promotion of agricultural diversification and in the movement from a largely subsistence to at least a partially cash economy. In so doing, rural seasonal unemployment also has been reduced and effective use of the agricultural work force increased. The total planted area has risen about 25 percent and, by 1962, agricultural production was expanding at about 4 percent per year. At the same time, the basic land ownership pattern which contributes so much to Thai stability has been preserved. Thus, some 85 to 89 percent of all Thai farmers still own their own land; and these holdings, which rarely exceed 10 acres, account for almost 90 percent of all land under cultivation. There continue to be, then, only a relatively few tenant farmers and farm laborers (the 1960 census listed 349,000 agricultural wage earners). In addition, despite the inadequacy of capital and credit facilities, the average indebtedness of the Thai farmer has remained relatively low (less than 3 percent of total assets according to a 1953 Food and Agriculture Organization survey).

As agricultural diversification and growth occurred after 1950, other structural modifications were stimulated throughout the economy. New demands arose for additional storage facilities, transportation, and communications; as well as for farm implements and fertilizers, food processing and canning plants, improved wholesale, retail, and banking facilities; and for more specialized public administrative structures to perform the related governmental functions. These new demands, as a result, helped to produce a situation in which the agricultural sector's share of the gross domestic product actually dropped during 1950–1960 from 55 percent to 36 percent, while those sectors which serviced the expanding agricultural production increased significantly both in absolute terms and in terms of their share of that product. As examples, one can cite the facts that, during 1950–1960, transportation, communication, and storage's share of the gross domestic product increased from 3.2 percent to 7 percent, while that of the related wholesale and retail trades increased from 13.6 percent to 14.5 percent and manufacturing increased from 11.5 percent to 14.5 percent.

In this process of modernizing agriculture and related service sectors from 1949 to 1961, it is of particular importance to note that Thai cultural and behavioral attitudes also were being modified. As in the previous century, a measure of cultural flexibility was again displayed as farmers and those involved in associated services continued to develop a greater appreciation for the potentialities of commercial activity. A willingness to pursue personal material rewards for successful efforts in the market economy was demonstrated. Although such movement away from the traditional subsistence agricultural economy did not involve a revolutionary behavioral transformation which saw huge numbers of Thai rushing into the urbanized industrial sectors, it did provide further documentation of the fact that the Thai are willing at least to engage in more modern cultivation and food processing activities when government provides them with guidance and some real help.

In the industrial and manufacturing sectors, however, as also noted earlier, there was much less success in development. No more than 15 percent of the gross domestic product and 19 percent of the gross national product was produced by these types of economic activities, with most manufacturing of any consequence being conducted by the 130 or so government enterprises (sawmills, cement, glass, sugar, tobacco, textiles, distilleries, etc.). Even these industries were and still are small in size, and are associated mainly with agricultural-product processing or with transportation, communications, electric power, and water supply systems. Private firms were generally even smaller in size, nonmodern in organization, and engaged chiefly in the production of light consumer goods, with many firms no more than family-operated handicraft and cottage industries. As a result, even now, there are only an estimated 1.5 percent of the total population and 3 percent of the economically active population who are engaged in all forms of business and industry, with the overwhelming majority of such workers being in the service rather than in the manufacturing sector. Moreover, an estimated 60 percent to 70 percent of the industrial work force is Chinese, and the percentage of skilled nonagricultural workers who are Chinese is even higher. Public employees, including workers in government enterprises, account for approximately one-third of all nonagricultural wage earners.

The accomplishments in economic growth and structural modification achieved between 1950 and the advent of the Sarit government in 1958, although significant, were not, as remarked earlier, the result of any all-out campaign by government. There was, indeed, a greater willingness to provide necessary economic leadership than had been true prior to World War II, but the efforts were fragmented, uneven, and not sustained with maximum energy. Since the 1958 coup d'etat, however, the new leadership has revealed a much greater preoccupation with the national requirements for economic development. Spurred in large measure by the deteriorating political situation in Southeast Asia and heightened Communist threats to national security, as well as by the extensive recommendations transmitted to it by a World Bank Survey Mission in 1959, Marshal Sarit launched a sustained effort to intensify and further rationalize the country's economic development programs. The stage was set by the "Supreme Commander," upon his personal assumption of power, in an address to his government's advisory National Economic Council, when he declared:

> The national economy is beset with difficulties; it is, therefore, time that something is done to save the beloved country from this plight and lead it on the path of welfare and prosperity. . . . All obstacles and impediments have, therefore, to be swept away.[5]

With this type of authoritative public acknowledgment of the need for further economic development, Thailand's leadership then began what was for the country a major, concerted attempt at planned improvement. The economic advisory council became a

[5] See the *Bangkok Post,* February 4, 1959.

National Economic Development Board, with Marshal Sarit as chairman, and was assigned the duty of formulating and supervising long-range development plans. Although the board's composition differed for political reasons from that recommended by the World Bank—which advised that it be composed of the appropriate Cabinet ministers—and instead was composed chiefly of military officers and civil servants plus a secretariat tied to the Prime Minister's office, it nevertheless provided a high-level mechanism at the center of national leadership. During 1959, moreover, a Board of Investment was created to supervise government regulations in this field and, simultaneously, to create new means for attracting investors. This step led to an Industrial Investment Act of October 1960, which was designed to provide significant incentives to investors in particular industries earmarked for development. Foreign investors were guaranteed protection from nationalization or from competition by public enterprise in specific industries, were given the right of unrestricted withdrawal of capital and profits from the country, and were exempted from income taxes for two to five years and from import duties on machinery. Finally the National Economic Development Board produced during 1960 the country's first economic development plan: a broad six-year program for the period 1961–1966, to be implemented in two stages. Subsequently, a second plan was created for the period 1967–1971.

THE ECONOMIC DEVELOPMENT PLANS

As one might expect in view of the fact that the post-1958 leadership has been drawn from the same elite as its predecessors, the general philosophy and objectives of the Thai Plans are moderately conservative and seek to be realistic. They are not ideologically doctrinaire, overly ambitious, or devoted to largely impractical objectives. No economic revolution has been blueprinted, no total transformation of the state and society has been sought, and no excessive stimulation of popular aspirations has been introduced. The Plans are, in fact, programmatic statements of objectives which remain rooted in the earlier economic policy positions previously identified. The strategy implied, therefore, contains few new and no radical components. The main value of the Plans, then, is that they constitute an effort by government to focus upon and specify Thai economic policy objectives and strategy, and to relate them to certain specific growth targets within a stated period of time.

The primary objective of the first Thai Plan "is to raise the living standard by mobilizing and utilizing both human and natural resources to achieve a high rate of economic growth." [6] However, as one qualified professional writer also has observed, "the special characteristic is an emphasis on the well-being, both material and spiritual, of the population." [7] As a consequence, no attempt is made to achieve the "practical maximum rate of investment" through the imposition on the population of consumer austerity in order to gain a higher future standard of living. In this connection, one can add that this approach reflects the leadership's continued lack of interest in Marxism, totalitarianism, and democratic socialism as well as its long-standing desire to avoid the creation of unmanageable social tensions.

Within this historic attitudinal framework, a number of economic development policies have been established which reveal the current Thai government's basic strategy. These policies and their objectives may be summarized as follows: [8]

[6] Vichitvong N. Pombhejara, "The Second Phase of Thailand's Six-Year Economic Development Plan, 1964–1966," *Asian Survey*, V, No. 3 (March 1965), 163. This article provides an excellent review of the Plan's strengths and weaknesses, which has been drawn upon in this discussion.

[7] *Ibid.*

[8] See Eliezer B. Ayal, "Thailand's Six-Year National Economic Development Plan," *Asian Survey*, I, No. 11 (January 1962), 33–42, for an excellent analysis which has been drawn upon heavily. Also, see D. C. Methi, "Thailand's First Six-Year Plan," *Eastern World*, XV, No. 4 (April 1961), 32–33; Bunchana Attakor, "National Economic Development Program," *Thai Journal of Public Administration*, I, No. 1 (July 1960), (in Thai); and Ayal, "Some Crucial Issues in Thailand's Economic Development," *Pacific Affairs*, XXXIV, No. 2 (Summer 1961), 157–164.

(1) *Financial Improvement and Budgetary Soundness*

At the outset, the first Plan was designed to assure the country's financial and budgetary soundness. It therefore continued to reflect the long-standing Thai emphasis on the maintenance of currency stability. This was to be perpetuated not only through the already existing Exchange Equalization Fund but also by increased taxation if the heavy new public expenditures for development began to produce serious inflationary pressures. Foreign aid and loans, moreover, were assumed to be an integral part of the program—a departure from pre-World War II reluctance to be dependent on foreign financial resources. In conjunction with budgetary reforms introduced in 1960 which brought the heavy budgetary deficits of the preceding decade under control, and the maintenance of price levels to annual increases of no more than 2 percent, the value of the *baht* has been protected effectively, to date, in accordance with this objective. Moreover, with an expansion of exports, foreign exchange reserves have been growing to a point where, by 1963, they were sufficient to pay for one year's imports. Although it was anticipated that capital imports would probably reduce this export surplus, a trade balance in terms of an annual 4 percent increase per year of both exports and imports was planned for 1963–1966.

Associated with this goal of financial soundness, the Plan sought an increase in the national budget from about 14 percent of gross national product to 15 percent of GNP plus the additional receipt of foreign and international aid on an order of 4,000 million *baht* in loans and 3,000 million *baht* in grants. (The *baht* was established by the International Monetary Fund at a par value of 20.84 per United States dollar.) Planned economic development budget expenditures from domestic sources were then to increase from 19 percent of the 1960 total budget to 28.7 percent in 1966. Once again, therefore, the Thai government was demonstrating its commitment to fiscal caution.

(2) *Economic Growth in Conjunction with
Improved Individual Income*

A second major objective of the 1961–1966 Plan was to increase both national and per capita income simultaneously. The Plan thus projected an average annual increase in national income of 5 percent, in contrast to the 4 percent of the preceding decade. At the same time, per capita income was to be increased from the previous 2 percent to at least 3 percent per year. By setting these twin objectives, the government was clearly attempting to promote both economic growth and immediate improvement in the personal economic condition of its citizens. Obviously, with a population expansion of about 3 percent per year, the accomplishment of these goals has depended heavily upon an expansion in productivity and in Thai export trade. It is hoped that the gross domestic product will double between 1961 and 1976.

Philosophically, these targets also reflected the government's aversion to the imposition of sacrifices upon the citizenry. There is neither a totalitarian nor even a social democratic or Fabian Socialist willingness to increase the rapidity of economic growth through maximized investment under programs of austerity and enforced savings. Early improvements in popular standards of living are desired even if the result is a slower rate of economic modernization and development.

(3) *Public Investment Primarily in Social
Overhead Capital*

The first Plan called for an increase in capital formation from the previous 14 to 15 percent to at least 15 percent. Economic development expenditures by government from domestic sources were planned to increase from 19.5 percent of the total government budget in 1961 to 28.7 percent of the budget in 1966. Reflecting both its own emphasis on the importance of private economic effort as well as the recommendations of the World Bank, the major public investment has been in such social overhead capital areas as power, transportation and communication, irrigation, public utilities, public health and education, and research. It has been hoped that through these public investments, economic development would be spurred, and the private sector would then be able to obtain maximum return from its own investment and effort. Thus, by the period 1964–1966, 35 percent of budgeted development expenditures were to be for communication and transportation, 9.2 percent for power and energy, 19.2 percent for education. All forms of transportation and communication also were to be greatly expanded and improved; electric power generation and distribution facilities were developed considerably; major investments in the improvement of irrigation systems were called for; heavy emphasis was placed on public health and education (including manpower training); agriculture was assisted not merely by improved irrigation but also by various extension activities and expanded credit and marketing cooperatives, as well as by agricultural research; resource development surveys were to be undertaken; and industry was to be aided by resource surveys, market research information, an expansion of credit facilities, and the identification and provision of industrial sites.

(4) *Commitment to Private Enterprise*

The first Plan's emphasis on public investment primarily in social overhead capital areas suggests the extent to which Thailand continues to be committed to a mixed economy in which the private sector is the major component. Agricultural, commercial, and industrial activities are being left primarily to private enterprise, with government serving mainly as overall coordinator, regulator, and facilitator. To this end, the various government enterprises are supposed to become self-supporting and independent of public subsidization; the Thai farmer hopefully will become less dependent upon middlemen (who are chiefly Chinese), not through increased dependence upon government but through his newer and better cooperatives and cultivation skills; and government will restrict itself in commercial and industrial activities primarily to the maintenance of standards and quality (particularly in exports) and to the preservation of proper price levels through a Warehouse Organization, which will buy and sell goods to achieve such price levels. Moreover, the government has become actively involved in the promotion of foreign private investment in the economy through the provision of various tax advantages and other inducements. In this way, too, therefore, the Thai economic development strategy is clearly one which emphasizes stimulation of and support for private entrepreneurial activity. This strategy reflects an historic policy attitude, the lack of success achieved by most of the industrial public enterprises created prior to 1958, and the shortage in skilled planning and managerial personnel.

(5) *Emphasis on Agricultural Modernization and Diversification*

As an overwhelmingly agricultural society with a large annual population growth rate, it is critical for Thailand to improve its agricultural sector. Moreover, since most of its exports are agricultural and limited chiefly to several products, it is also essential to engage in agricultural diversification. The first Plan has sought to meet these needs to some extent. The heavy investment in irrigation and power as well as the other forms of assistance to the farmer have already been noted. In toto, they were to amount to 15.3 percent of the budgetary expenditures for the period 1964–1966. An overall annual increase of 3 percent in agricultural production was planned from the outset; and, in the interest of diversification and export market opportunities, maize production was scheduled to be doubled, tapioca production to be increased by 15 percent, and fishing to be increased by 50 percent during the first three years. Rubber production, however, was to increase by 6 percent by the end of the initial three-year period while rice was scheduled for an annual expansion of only 1.3 percent. On the other hand, since the Plan also recognized the need for some structural modifications in the economy, agriculture's share in the rising gross domestic product (expected to increase by 6 percent per year) was expected to continue to decline. It was 36 percent in 1960 but probably was only 33 percent in 1966. A decline at this rate presumably would still allow for a 4 percent per year growth in exports.

(6) *Encouragement of Private Investment in Manufacturing*

The first Plan projected an increase in the value of mining and industrial production from an annual rate of 10 percent to 12 percent, with the increases being obtained primarily by the expanded extraction of tin ore, lignite, gypsum and the increased production of tobacco, cement, gunny sacks, textiles, and paper. As already noted, government's role in this growth was to be as a facilitator of private investment and effort. Manufacturing and mining, therefore, were scheduled to obtain only 6.1 percent of budgeted expenditures for economic development during 1964–1966, in contrast to the far higher figures for social capital and agriculture. It was hoped that by this combination of government facilitation and private entrepreneurship, mining, manufacturing, and construction would increase their share of the gross domestic product from 19 percent in 1961 to 21 percent in 1966, at the same time that agriculture's share would drop by 4 percent. This adjustment would constitute a structural modification in the interest of greater economic balance and would be obtained in an atmosphere of absolute economic growth by all sectors. Nevertheless, it also was clearly to be a limited and gradual structural transformation. There is no evidence in Thai government planning of any major effort to industrialize.

(7) *Regionalism*

Incorporated within the first Plan was an awareness of the need for regionally balanced growth. The specific economic development requirements of each of the major regions were therefore taken into consideration. These several regional programs, with their differing emphases, have been supervised by special committees headed by Cabinet members, with national coordination provided by the National Economic Development Board Secretariat. This aspect of the Plan was both economically sound and also essential to national security, as the special development efforts currently required in the Northeast demonstrate. Regional differences in the country certainly are sufficiently great to warrant such special administrative and programming attention.

The Results of the First Plan

During 1966, the Office of the National Economic Development Board issued a preliminary review and evaluation of the results of the first Plan. Its conclusion was that the targets were achieved in almost all sectors. In general, this conclusion seems to be borne out by the still fragmentary statistics available. Thus, for example, further progress toward the objective of fiscal and budgetary soundness has been recorded. There has been an average annual growth in GNP of 6 to 7 percent at the same time that government revenues have increased annually by about 11 percent; the latter increase is a product in large measure of improved tax collection efficiency under a program developed in conjunction with the United States Agency for International Development. This has been accomplished despite the fact that there still has been no major change in relationships among revenue sources —customs continuing to produce the largest share ($207 million out of $464 million in 1964 and $258 million out of $577 million in 1966).

While government revenues and the GNP were increasing in this fashion, price levels were held in check; the consumer price index for all items in Bangkok and Thonburi rising by a total of no more than 7.7 percent from 1962 to 1966. Gold reserves also continued to rise and were about $600 million by 1965 as compared to about $300 million in 1956, with 1966 hard currency reserves estimated at about $640 million. The Thai *baht,* therefore, is one of the "hardest" currencies of Southeast Asia. Of the estimated GNP of $3.6 billion in 1965, government budget expenditures represented some 16 percent.

In regard to the goal of associating economic growth with improved individual income, it has been estimated by private international business sources operating in Thailand that, despite the population growth, the individual Thai's *real* income has probably risen by as much as 80 percent since 1955, with most of this occurring since 1961. With productivity increased and inflation held in check, the "real" annual per capita GNP is probably about $203 despite the "money" per capita figure hovering about $101. In percentage terms, per capita "money" income probably has been increasing at the 4 percent per year rate envisioned.

In a similar vein, public investment in social overhead capital has been expanded sufficiently to produce significant improvements. Installed power generating capacity has almost doubled from its 286,630 kilowatts in 1961 to 554,260 kilowatts in 1965. Road mileage also increased by an estimated 7.4 percent from 1961 to 1965 while railway mileage expanded by about 3 percent in the same period. In addition to such major power and irrigation complexes as the Yanhee Project completed in 1964, a number of diversion canals have been constructed to increase the total amount of arable land. Communications facilities, too, have been improved with the addition of new radio relay stations which reach deep into the rural areas and new television stations covering the metropolitan areas of the eight largest cities. The government also reported greater success during 1965 in mobilizing domestic financial resources for development expenditures than had been previously the case. Moreover, continued expansion of educational, health, and welfare facilities has also occurred under the stimulation of expanded public investment. In education, enrollments generally have continued to rise in all schools, as have the numbers of teachers. In public health, there are now more hospitals and clinics than ever before, with medical centers now established in all districts and new mobile medical units operating in rural regions like the Northeast.

The operation of the first Plan also has produced structural modifications of the economy as well as an enhancement of productivity. Thus, mining, manufacturing, and construction are now accounting for about 19 percent of gross domestic product although agriculture, forestry, and fishing still account for 34 percent and trade, communications, finance, utilities, etc. (tertiary industries) about 47 percent. As to production, the absolute figures reveal steady expansion of all forms of crop production, with particularly notable increases in rubber, maize, sugar, kenaf and tobacco while rice production continued to rise at a far slower rate from 1961 to 1966. In the case of minerals, tin concentrates, wolfram concentrates, lead ore, antimony ore, iron ore, manganese, fluorite, and lignite all recorded major increases. Although the balance-of-trade has remained unfavorable (a negative balance of 3,244,519,000 *baht* in 1965 compared to a negative balance in 1963 of 3,126,464,000 *baht*), absolute figures expanded considerably—imports totaling, in value, 16,185,331,000 *baht* in 1965 as compared to 12,802,765,000 *baht* in 1963 while exports rose from 9,676,301,000 *baht* in 1963 to 12,940,812,000 *baht* by 1965.

In sum, and without belaboring statistics which are necessarily fragmentary, Thailand has generally been making good economic progress since 1961 and it has been doing it largely in Thai fashion and for Thai objectives. It seems likely that, all other things being equal, the second Plan will help to continue this progress in economic growth, diversification, and careful structural reform. It, too, places its "primary emphasis . . . on the development of intensive agriculture, raising productivity by greater use of capital and improved techniques, as a means to provide food and employment for a growing population, to provide basic materials for an expanding industry and to provide foreign exchange for the payment of imports." [9] This improvement in agricultural productivity is to occur in conjunction with continued concern for the mainte-

[9] See The National Economic Development Board, *The Second Five Year Plan [1967–1971]* (Bangkok, 1966).

nance of financial solvency, government "provision of necessary economic infrastructures and healthy environment" for "private enterprise," without interfering or competing unduly in business and industry, due concern for gearing such development to national security requirements, and with an effort to reduce existing inequalities in income and social benefits both generally and particularly in the case of current geographic imbalances. There is evidence of intention to accelerate rural development, to focus on regional development outside the Central Plain, and to involve local administration more directly and to a greater degree in the actual conduct of economic growth, public welfare, and community development projects.

The actions outlined in the two Plans are necessary not only for continued Thai viability as a country but also in terms of the security problems previously discussed. Certainly, the socioeconomic structures and statistics which characterize the Thai Northeast must be greatly improved if the material sources of discontent and alienation are to be eliminated: a rural income only 65 percent that of the rest of the country, a greater discrepancy in income among farmers than elsewhere (the upper 2 percent receiving 10 times more cash than the lowest 78 percent), and an estimated total annual per capita income in the lowest group of about $30.[10] But then, since both development and defense are only partially economic problems, the political, social, and cultural problems of that same region—as with all of Thailand —also must be treated effectively.[11]

Thai Development Strategy and the Problems of National Security: A Critique

Contemporary Thai development policies and strategy, both before and under the two development Plans, have been devoted

[10] See Millard F. Long, "Economic Development in Northeast Thailand: Problems and Prospects," *Asian Survey*, VI, No. 7 (July 1966), 355–356.
[11] See "Symposium on Northeast Thailand," *ibid.*, pp. 349–380.

primarily to the conservative management of economic growth and structural modification. The strategy now being employed is one which is rooted in historic policy attitudes as well as in the nonsocialist recommendations of the World Bank and the United States: major direct public investment in social overhead capital, with particular emphasis on education; continued concern for the improvement and modernization of the traditional agricultural sector; encouragement of gradual expansion of the industrial sector through private investment (domestic and foreign); maintenance of Thai financial and monetary stability. The result has been some significant economic progress which, in the view of several observers, has placed Thailand in the position of approaching self-supporting economic growth. Operating within the framework of the Plans and with the help of substantial foreign aid and technical assistance, new roads have been built, hydro-electric power and irrigation facilities significantly expanded, agricultural diversification continued, and rice crop yields somewhat increased. Significant success in negotiating foreign loans for capital investment has been achieved, and there has been a steady increase in the number of firms which have signed contracts under the Industrial Investment Act, including Thai and Chinese firms. The response of private investors, both local and foreign, therefore, generally has been positive. Moreover, while a higher rate of development expenditures and economic growth has been obtained during the first Plan, and a stronger balance of payments position achieved, domestic price levels and monetary stability also have been preserved.

On the other hand, current Thai economic growth is not without its problems, both substantive and managerial. In the critical area of investment policy, for example, the provision of legal inducements to foreign investors and the general willingness to see private enterprise play a major role in the economy represent a realization of the valuable economic and social contributions which can be made by these groups. However, serious questions can be raised about the extent to which the resultant capital formation and rate of investment in economic development actually will be sufficient. The growth of domestic Thai capital formation remains slow, and there continues to be reluctance on the part both of local and foreign investors to engage in truly productive long-term investment. The manufacturing sector is still extremely small and dominated by primary-product processing activities conducted on a small-scale basis. Government, therefore, may have to play a more vigorous planning and investment role than is now contemplated if adequate amounts of capital are to be directed into appropriately diversified industrial development. Some development economists estimate that the actual rate of investment must be about 25 percent of national income in order to achieve a 5 percent increase in per capita income, if one takes into account the need to spend 2 to 4 percent just to offset a 1 percent increase in the population, another 2 to 4 percent for each 1 percent of increase in the per capita income, and 10 percent for public health, education, etc.

The growth of savings and capital, moreover, as well as its constructive employment for economic development, requires the creation of certain efficient institutions and procedures (e.g., a substantial banking system, a properly structured and enforced tax system, and various corporative devices). While some official reform efforts have been made in these areas, the Thai tax and customs structures still require a general overhaul, and savings and investment devices such as the government's Savings Bank or the government-supported but privately owned Industrial Finance Corporation have not yet been developed satisfactorily.

In the same vein, although positive steps have been taken to encourage necessary agricultural diversification, scientific agriculture is in its infancy. Overall agricultural productivity remains low and a major increase in the efficiency of rice production is still to be made. Further exploration and development of natural resources also is required. Similarly, although the education system is expanding in commendable fashion, it remains seriously deficient in quality and in the opportunities provided for scientific and technical training. Secondary and university graduates with these skills are not available in sufficient numbers to staff a modernizing economy. Moreover, there are significant cultural and social obstacles even to their effective employment.

The considerable expansion of government efforts to create adequate social overhead capital is also praiseworthy and can make a major contribution to future economic development, as can the improvement of public health and sanitation. Nevertheless, the need for additional major government investment in these areas indicates that Thailand is still struggling to establish some of the basic preconditions for real economic takeoff. Transportation and communication systems are not yet efficient, a further major expansion of power and energy resources is still needed, and the operating costs of all of these must be reduced. The same weakness is indicated by the extent to which the economically active population remains overwhelmingly committed—occupationally, culturally, and psychologically—to agriculture, while not yet engaging in it in "scientific" or "modern" fashion.

In other words, while the Thai government has conciously been taking some necessary and worthwhile steps in recent years to promote economic growth, it certainly has not been engaging in any massive modernization of the economy. Moreover, as some analysts have noted, even its economic planning methods may be criticized because they are mainly based upon "project analysis" and sectoral planning, rather than being comprehensive and implemented by modern programming techniques. It is, of course, true that the Thai are in the fortunate position of presently being able to subsist in adequate fashion (in Asian terms) without engaging in major and immediate economic transformations. Nevertheless, the pressures of population growth and export uncertainties, when combined with the rising economic aspirations of many citizens, are not really being greatly outstripped by development efforts, as yet. A tremendous amount remains to be done. Foreign aid and technical assistance assuredly can help, and the

Thai government obviously is planning on the continuation and even the expansion of this help. But the capital and the materiel and the skills which it can bring to Thailand can have major impact only as the Thai are willing and able to utilize them effectively. To date, there has been only a modest demonstration of these qualities by people and government, although more serious concern for economic growth has been evidenced in official circles in recent years than was previously true in any but the Pridi governments.

Socially as well as economically, moreover, Thailand still faces the fact that it has not yet clearly developed and identified, let alone empowered, a suitable Thai "pioneer" group. Without such a group, which would be completely willing to and capable of providing vigorous economic development leadership, major changes are not likely. Outside of the Chinese business community, the only consequential managerial group available in the society is still the government bureaucracy; and, as has been emphasized, this group has not yet demonstrated a vigorous developmental orientation while, in the past, it has actually performed poorly when involved in the management of public enterprises.

Not only is Thailand still lacking in an appropriate, skilled, innovative, and entrepreneurial group to lead the way, economically and socially, but, as has also been stressed, no significant transformation of the political system has yet occurred, either. W. W. Rostow's observation about the role of the polity in development thus becomes particularly appropriate to Thailand:

> Until a definitive political transformation occurs—which harnesses national energies, talents, and resources around the concrete tasks of economic growth—the take-off is likely to be postponed; negatively, because the thin layer of modern technical and administrative talent in the society (as well as the society's margin of savings) is likely to be dissipated in activities of low or negative productivity; positively, because the government is unlikely to play its role effectively in the

three sectoral developments—in social overhead capital, agriculture, and trade—necessary to create the matrix for sustained industrial growth.[12]

In sum, the assets of Thailand—its productive soil, agriculturally suitable climate, reasonably well-integrated majority, cultural flexibility, popular respect for authority, large and experienced bureaucracy—have produced a natural stability and have relieved government of many pressures in the past. But these assets have not been properly or fully harnessed by government in behalf of development. Unless the political system is actively popularized (although not necessarily immediately democratized), the administrative system significantly modernized, and the bureaucracy committed to broad-gauge development, controlled but successful development will not occur to the extent required, given the pressures which are building up and the dimensions of the national need. The result of this leadership failure will then be a steady weakening of respect for government as well as a weakening of societal stability, not just in regions like the Northeast or South but throughout the whole country. In the long run, Thai national independence and well-being will be endangered.

The bureaucratized Thai ruling elite, therefore, with its monopoly of power and its great authority, must provide the necessary vigorous leadership in behalf of national development; and it must define such development in political, social, and cultural as well as in economic terms. It must utilize its country's many natural and human assets, its own potential ability to serve effectively as the pioneer group if it so wishes, and foreign assistance; or it must face the responsibility for contributing to unnecessary national suicide. There must be "a definitive social, political and cultural victory of those who would modernize . . . over those who would cling to the traditional society or seek other goals." [13] Foreign aid can encourage and assist such modernizers but it

[12] W. W. Rostow, *The Stages of Economic Growth* (Cambridge: Cambridge University Press, 1960), pp. 143–144.

[13] *Ibid.*, p. 58.

cannot, in itself, create them; and it certainly cannot place them in the right positions within an alien society.

The Communist revolutionary challenge in the Thai border areas must indeed be faced, too. Violence must be contained and security provided the local populace. Improvement in the economic conditions of these regions must also be registered in a hurry. But, in addition to such military and economic efforts, these regions, with their ethnically distinct peoples, must also be effectively politicized—fully incorporated into the Thai state and culture as citizens who are willing to accept responsibility toward the preservation and prosperity of Thailand as well as to accept new benefits from it. Only in this way can revolutionary war be won by an existing regime, for such war is, first and foremost, "political." Thailand, as a whole, therefore, must intensify and broaden its development efforts in all respects while, simultaneously, providing special help in its immediately threatened regions so that they can both catch up to the rest of the country and then participate in its further advances.

Is Thailand going to be another Vietnam? It does not have to be, as its many assets and strengths indicate. But it may nevertheless become one. As an essentially administrative state governed by a conservative bureaucracy, it may not be able to rise to the new challenges sufficiently because to do so requires a major and rapid self-transformation in the ruling oligarchy. One can only hope that the Communist pressure is limited enough, the traditional Thai cultural resistances to revolution still strong enough, the education of new bureaucrats modern enough, and the dedication of senior Thai elites to their country great enough to produce in time that societal development (above and beyond limited economic growth) which alone can prevent still another agonizing Southeast Asia catastrophe.

SELECTED BIBLIOGRAPHY

BOOKS AND MONOGRAPHS

Blanchard, Wendell *et al. Thailand: Its People, Its Society, Its Culture.* Human Relations Area Files, Country Survey Series. New Haven: HRAF Press, 1958.

Bowring, Sir John. *The Kingdom and People of Siam.* 2 vols. London: J. W. Parker and Sons, 1857.

Busch, Noel F. *Thailand, an Introduction to Modern Siam.* Princeton: D. Van Nostrand Company, 1959.

Coast, John. *Some Aspects of Siamese Politics.* New York: Institute of Pacific Relations, 1953.

Darling, Frank C. *Thailand and the United States.* Washington, D.C.: Public Affairs Press, 1965.

de Young, John E. *Village Life in Modern Thailand.* Berkeley: University of California Press, 1958.

Excell, F. K. *The Land and People of Thailand.* New York: The Macmillan Company, 1960.

Hanna, Willard A. *Thailand's Strategic Northeast.* Southeast Asia Series, Vol. XIV, No. 1. New York: American Universities Field Staff, 1966.

Ingram, James C. *Economic Change in Thailand since 1850.* Stanford: Stanford University Press, 1955.

Insor, D. *Thailand.* New York: Frederick A. Praeger, Inc., 1963.

International Bank for Reconstruction and Development. *A Public Development Program for Thailand.* Baltimore: Johns Hopkins Press, 1959.

Landon, Kenneth P. *Siam in Transition.* Chicago: University of Chicago Press, 1939.

Moffat, Abbot L. *Mongkut, The King of Siam.* Ithaca: Cornell University Press, 1961.

Nuechterlein, Donald E. *Thailand and the Struggle for Southeast Asia.* Ithaca: Cornell University Press, 1965.

Pendleton, Robert L. *Thailand: Aspects of Landscape and Life.* New York: Duell, Sloan and Pearce, 1962.

Phillips, Herbert P. *Thai Peasant Personality.* Berkeley: University of California Press, 1965.

Riggs, Fred W. *Thailand: The Modernization of a Bureaucratic Polity.* Honolulu: East-West Center Press, 1966.

Sharp, Lauriston, ed. *Thailand.* New Haven: Human Relations Area Files, Inc., 1956.

Siffin, William J. *The Thai Bureaucracy: Institutional Change and Development.* Honolulu: East-West Center Press, 1966.

Skinner, G. William. *Leadership and Power in the Chinese Community of Thailand.* Ithaca: Cornell University Press, 1958.

Suriyabongse, Dr. Luang. *Buddhism in Thailand.* Bangkok: Phrae Bhithaya Co., n.d.

Sutton, Joseph L., ed. *Problems of Politics and Administration in Thailand.* Bloomington: Indiana University Press, 1962.

Vella, Walter F. *The Impact of the West on Government in Thailand.* Berkeley: University of California Press, 1955.

Wilson, David A. *Politics in Thailand.* Ithaca: Cornell University Press, 1962.

Wit, Daniel. *Labor Law and Practice in Thailand.* Washington, D.C.: U.S. Department of Labor, Bureau of Labor Statistics, BLS Report No. 267, 1964.

ARTICLES

Ayal, Eliezer B. "Some Crucial Issues in Thailand's Economic Development," *Pacific Affairs,* XXXIV (1961), 157–164.

Ayal, Eliezer B. "Thailand's Six Year National Economic Development Plan," *Asian Survey,* I (1962), 33–43.

Damrong, Rachanuphap, Prince. "The Introduction of Western Culture in Siam," *Journal of the Siam Society,* XX (October, 1926), 89–100.

Darling, Frank C. "American Policy in Thailand," *Western Political Quarterly,* XV (March 1962), 93–110.

Embee, John F. "Thailand—A Loosely-Structured Social System," *American Anthropologist,* LII (1950), 181–193.

Hughes, John. "Reds Aim at Thai Soft Spot," *Christian Science Monitor* (May 6, 1965), 1:2, 6:3.

Hughes, John. "Thailand Feels Red Pressure," *Christian Science Monitor* (April 21, 1965), 5:1.

King, John Kerry. "Thailand's Bureaucracy and the Threat of Communist Subversion," *Far Eastern Survey,* XXIII, No. 11 (1954), 169–173.

Kroessen, Lt. Colonel Frederik J. United States Army. "The Precarious Position of Thailand," *Military Review,* XLIV, No. 12 (December 1964), 63–69.

Mosel, James. "Thai Administrative Behavior," in William Siffin, *Toward the Comparative Study of Public Administration.* Bloomington: Indiana University, Department of Government, 1957.

Pombhejara, Vichitvong N. "The Second Phase of Thailand's Six-Year Economic Development Plan, 1964–1966," *Asian Survey,* V, No. 3, 161–168.

Sharp, Lauriston. "Peasants and Politics in Thailand," *Far Eastern Survey,* XIX, No. 15 (September 13, 1950), 157–161.

Shor, Edgar L. "The Thai Bureaucracy," *Administrative Science Quarterly,* V, No. 1 (June 1960), 66–86.

Skinner, G. William. "Chinese Assimilation and Thai Politics," *Journal of Asian Studies,* XVI (February 1957), 237–250.

Warner, Denis. "Thailand: Peking's New Front," *Reporter,* XXXII, No. 12 (June 17, 1965), 32–34.

Wilson, David A. "Thailand and Marxism." in Frank Trager, *Marxism in Southeast Asia.* Stanford: Stanford University Press, 1959.

Wilson, David A. "The Military in Thai Politics," in J. J. Johnson, ed., *The Role of the Military in Underdeveloped Countries.* Princeton: Princeton University Press, 1962.

INDEX

197